MANAGING THE
ACADEMIC UNIT

**Managing Universities and Colleges:
Guides to Good Practice**

Series editors:

David Warner, Principal and Chief Executive, Swansea Institute of Higher Education

David Palfreyman, Bursar and Fellow, New College, Oxford

This series has been commissioned in order to provide systematic analysis of the major areas of the management of colleges and universities, emphasizing good practice.

Current titles
Allan Bolton: *Managing the Academic Unit*
Judith Elkin and Derek Law (eds): *Managing Information*
John M. Gledhill: *Managing Students*
Christine Humfrey: *Managing International Students*
Colleen Liston: *Managing Quality and Standards*

Forthcoming titles include
Ann Edworthy: *Managing Stress*
David Nicol: *Managing Learning and Teaching*
Andrew Paine: *Managing Hospitality Services*
Harold Thomas: *Managing Financial Resources*
David Watson: *Managing Strategy*

MANAGING THE ACADEMIC UNIT

Allan Bolton

2000

Open University Press
Buckingham · Philadelphia

Open University Press
Celtic Court
22 Ballmoor
Buckingham
MK18 1XW

e-mail: enquiries@openup.co.uk
world wide web: http://www.openup.co.uk

and
325 Chestnut Street
Philadelphia, PA 19106, USA

First Published 2000

A catalogue record of this book is available from the British Library

ISBN   0 335 20404 X (hb)   0 335 20403 1 (pb)

Library of Congress Cataloging-in-Publication Data
Bolton, Allan.
    Managing the academic unit / Allan Bolton.
        p.   cm. – (Managing universities and colleges)
    Includes bibliographical references (p.   ) and index.
    ISBN 0-335-20404-X. – ISBN 0-335-20403-1 (pbk.)
    1. Departmental chairmen (Universities) – Great Britain.   2. Deans
(Education) – Great Britain.   3. College administrators – Great
Britain.   4. Universities and colleges – Great Britain
– Administration.   I. Title.   II. Series.
LB2341.B583   2000
378.1′11–dc21   99-16160
                                                              CIP

Typeset by Graphicraft Limited, Hong Kong
Printed in Great Britain by The Cromwell Press, Trowbridge

CONTENTS

9   Benchmarking   127

10   Preparing to lead, manage – and depart   134

SERIES EDITORS' INTRODUCTION

Post-secondary educational institutions can be viewed from a variety of different perspectives. For the majority of students and staff who work in them, they are centres of learning and teaching where the participants are there by choice and consequently, by and large, work very hard. Research has always been important in some higher education institutions, but in recent years this emphasis has grown and what for many was a great pleasure and, indeed, a treat is becoming more of a threat and an insatiable performance indicator which just has to be met. Maintaining the correct balance between quality research and learning/teaching, while the unit of resource continues to decline inexorably, is one of the key issues facing us all. Educational institutions as workplaces must be positive and not negative environments.

From another aspect, post-secondary educational institutions are clearly communities, functioning to all intents and purposes like small towns and internally requiring and providing a similar range of services, while also having very specialist needs. From yet another, they are seen as external suppliers of services to industry, commerce and the professions. These 'customers' receive, *inter alia*, a continuing flow of well-qualified fresh graduates with transferable skills, part-time and short course study opportunities through which to develop existing employees, consultancy services to solve problems and help expand business, and research and development support to create new breakthroughs.

However, educational institutions are also significant businesses in their own right. One recent study of the economic impact of higher education in Wales shows that it is of similar importance in employment terms to the steel or banking/finance sectors. Put another way, Welsh higher education institutions (HEIs) spend half a billion pounds annually and create more than 23,000 full-time equivalent jobs. And it must be remembered that there are only 13 HEIs in Wales, compared with 171 in the whole of the UK, and that these Welsh institutions are, on average, relatively small. In addition, it has recently been realized that UK higher education is a major export industry with the added benefit of long-term financial and political returns. If the UK further education sector is added to this equation, then the economic impact of post-secondary education is of truly startling proportions.

Whatever perspective you take, it is obvious that educational institutions require managing and, consequently, this series has been produced to facilitate that end. The editors have striven to identify authors who are distinguished practitioners in their own right and can also write. The authors have been given the challenge of producing essentially practical handbooks which combine appropriate theory and contextual material with many examples of good practice and guidance.

The topics chosen are of key importance to educational management and stand at the forefront of current debate. Some of these topics have never been covered in depth before and all of them are equally applicable to further as well as higher education. The editors are firmly of the belief that the UK distinction between these sectors will continue to blur and will be replaced, as in many other countries, by a continuum where the management issues are entirely common.

For well over a decade, both of the editors have been involved with a management development programme for senior staff from HEIs throughout the world. Every year the participants quickly learn that we share the same problems and that similar solutions are normally applicable. Political and cultural differences may on occasion be important, but are often no more than an overlying veneer. Hence, this series will be of considerable relevance and value to post-secondary educational managers in many countries.

We are pleased that this fourth volume in the series covers a much neglected area of management which is, nevertheless, common to almost all educational institutions. The 'academic unit' may be a somewhat clumsy description, but the reality it describes, (known variously as 'faculty', 'school', 'department', 'programme area' and so on) is for many the very heart and soul of educational organizations. This book has been written by someone on the inside who has thought long and hard about the various issues involved and it shows. Every chapter is full of insights and practical advice which will help both academic and administrative staff involved in the day to day management of an academic unit.

It is perhaps appropriate that Allan Bolton should work in a business school, for such units have been in the forefront of the arguments for as much independence as possible from the 'centre'. This desire to go it alone has almost certainly been strengthened by the tendency of many senior managers to use business schools as milch cows to subsidize other, less favoured units. Allan's base at Lancaster University has also enabled him to draw upon that institution's entertaining Innovation in Higher Education series for several apposite illustrations and anecdotes.

David Warner
David Palfreyman

LIST OF BOXES
AND TABLES

PREFACE AND ACKNOWLEDGEMENTS

The impetus to create this book came from a research project undertaken in 1991 with the aid of a Fulbright Fellowship. The main subject of that study, strategic development of selected business schools in the US, diversified into another research project on leadership in academic units with reference to business schools in the US, UK and continental Europe.

The groundwork for the book is based upon experience since 1976 in administration and management at the universities of Warwick and Lancaster, acting on behalf of faculties of arts, science, educational studies, a department of continuing education and a school of management. For much of the time, combining that work with a central registry function, when one acts on behalf of the institution as a whole, has added an element of tension that has occasionally been creative. That tension is in large part the subject of this book.

My thanks go to colleagues and counterparts with whom I have compared experiences, to academic leaders whose wisdom and energy have made my efforts worthwhile, and to administrators whose professionalism and creativity have inspired me.

Particular thanks for helping in the creation of this book are due to Dennis Jones, Professor Jim Campbell and Jenny Hocking at Warwick, to Malcolm Everett at Birmingham, Roddy Livingston at Strathclyde, Michael Ambler at City, Sue Gemmill at Surrey, Jane Filby at Aston, Lee Taylor at The Open University and to Claire O'Donnell, who has done a long and admirable job in producing the material in presentable form.

1

A WORLD OF CHANGE

Much has been written about the challenges of managing universities and colleges, hereafter referred to collectively as HEIs (higher education institutions). Some important publications are listed in the Bibliography but most of them tend to approach the challenges from a central institutional perspective. The environment is often analysed at the level of whole institutions, their decision-making structures and leading officers. When the constituent parts of HEIs are mentioned, it is often to illustrate the diversity, peculiarity or anarchic nature of those parts. They tend to be framed as part of the problem rather than part of the solution.

This book is an attempt, overdue in my opinion, to redress the balance of attention between 'the centre' and the academic units. 'Academic unit' is a term intended to cover units, departments, schools and faculties. Apart from being inelegant, the term is simplistic in that it implies an essential 'sameness' as if good generalizations might apply equally to a research centre in the economics of public transport, to a department of chemistry, and to a faculty of catering, tourism and leisure management. This point is more important than it seems because so much argument within HEIs is about the appropriate location of decision making and operations. For example, it may not be a matter of whether or not there should be an open day, but of whether there should be one organized in each faculty, or indeed one per department.

The scope of this book is intended to reach into further education, into countries throughout the world and across the full range of subjects. The choice of examples tends to reflect my own experience and readers are encouraged to look to the underlying arguments for relevance to their own position. Such situations are liable to change, for example as the boundaries between higher education and further education become less distinct, as we are positively encouraged to work across international boundaries and as strategies applied in a particular subject area or nation are adopted and adapted by others.

The decline of centralization

In a rational desire for control and orderliness, central officers have wished the academic units to be either organizationally weak, so that they depend upon central services, *or* well disciplined in a small number of relatively large units, so as to shorten lines of communication. In the first case, a well-resourced centre has permitted only a minimum of local support so that these disempowered units would have to be organized through the services granted to them by the centre. Some have been virtually powerless to do more than make requests across the range of their functions – from marketing themselves, appointing staff, admitting students, through running exams, booking rooms and writing cheques to painting walls and emptying bins. Powerful forces now act against such a set-up. Pressure to reduce budgets makes some central officers wish to off-load tasks on to the academic units and to eliminate communications with many separate departments. Since the late 1980s the rate in the growth of student numbers, outpacing growth in academic and administrative staffing, has made it more difficult to run wholly centralized systems, so that managing two thousand students in each of nine faculties on three campuses is seen as preferable to managing all eighteen thousand at one central point. Such forces have shifted us much closer to the second scenario envisaged above: a central administration with a stake in working with nine professionally organized faculty offices rather than with sixty disempowered departments. A registrar undergoing the stresses of acting as the HEI's returning officer for the Research Assessment Exercise (RAE) will sleep better for knowing that the nine offices are checking the data and completing the forms on behalf of the sixty departments. The disorganized, the late, the recalcitrant and the vague can be transformed within a group with a span of control of seven to one; not so at a ratio of sixty to a remotely located one!

Wishful thinking has caused some central officers to expect too much of the devolved model. It is convenient for them to assume that a report from a dean of a faculty reflects exactly the combined view and guaranteed cooperation of all the staff concerned, or that the dean who is sent away to implement a 10 per cent reduction in budget will be able to make it stick. The academic units are still subject to those same characteristics which are the traditional glory and curse of universities.

Management skills for academia ■

Research repeatedly confirms the everyday experience of those involved that management in higher education is both more satisfying and more difficult than managing in industry. More satisfying in that one is dealing with highly intelligent people, most of whom are motivated by the intrinsic attractions of their work rather than by prospects of short-term bonuses or promotion. More difficult in that those same people do not typically expect to behave in response to instructions from a line manager – an expression rarely used in higher education – nor to be motivated primarily by the corporate goals of the unit or institution. These generalizations were strongly underlined by my research interviewing deans of business schools in the US, continental Europe and the UK who had held careers both in industry and in higher education. More subtle skills of management and leadership and longer time-scales are required in academia (Bolton 1996).

Some of those skills are indicated in Colin Carnall's *Managing Change in Organizations* (Carnall 1990: 26–7) in which he deals with the special needs of professionals in organizations. It is interesting to note that some features of his description reveal the desirability of their operating within devolved, decentralized systems – comparable with the academic unit which is the subject of this book.

Increasingly, organizations manage professionals on the following principles:

1 *Emphasizing decentralization*: managers depend on the contribution, effort and skills of the professional employee. Thus motivation and control are sensitive issues and too much direction can be counterproductive. Managers tend to share responsibility and the professional has to learn to take responsibility for management decisions and how to communicate with management. Examples include the growing input into management of doctors in the healthcare field and of data-processing specialists and marketing specialists in corporate management.
2 *Depending less on 'rational' controls*: too much concern and reliance on quantitative measures can lead to unintended consequences. That does not mean that less monitoring and planning is needed. Quite the opposite! However, performance review is carried out with, rather than on, professionals. Involvement is important

because judgement in handling a range of quantitative and qualitative measures becomes important.

3 *Placing greater emphasis on intrinsic motivation*: in particular career development seems to be of great importance, and attention must therefore be paid to delegation, challenge, training and development as well as to motivators such as pay, status, and so on.

4 *Placing greater emphasis on team working*: different professional groups will hold and argue strongly for their own diverse views. Thus professional organizations must handle conflict. People skills and team-building skills are therefore of great importance.

5 *Placing more emphasis on conflict management*: the conflict referred to above needs to be managed. Uncertainty and complex tasks create the conditions for conflict, along with the point made under (4) above. Management need to keep in close touch with the various professional groups, and use team-building and involvement to communicate decisions quickly and effectively. All these are means of handling conflict constructively.

6 *Using matrix management and project structures*: there is a real need to create structures which place primary emphasis on the work to be done and how to provide for the contribution of different professional groups to that work. These structures emphasize task or team cultures. The various professional groups will be interdependent, thus emphasizing the need for matrix or project (task force) approaches to planning and to management.

7 *Placing more emphasis on trust*: trust is difficult to establish. Managers, other employees and clients place trust in professionals. This creates great pressure for consistency and fairness in the management of organizations; without it some stakeholders may become dissatisfied. There will still be organizational politics but for these to be constructively managed they need to be surrounded by a reasonable degree of openness.

8 *Placing more emphasis on values and ethics*: top management devotes considerable time and energy to articulating the organization's mission, values and ethics. It cannot control professionals directly and thus codes of behaviour conducive to trusting relationships are very important. This should be a joint management and professional task. Often it is neglected because it does not solve everyday issues and problems. Nevertheless, longer run success seems to depend on greater self-regulation within professional organizations.

Comparing the management of HEIs with the management of commercial organizations has become a frequent, though rarely systematic, exercise. Just as those in higher education were being urged to become more professional and 'managerial', for example by the Jarratt Report (1985), pressures developed in a different direction as management practitioners and writers advocated a move away from monolithic corporate cultures towards greater 'empowerment' at the local level. A danger was identified, for example by Middlehurst (1993), that HEIs were about to become more like businesses just as businesses began to see commercial advantages in the valuing of individuals and of collegiality traditionally associated with the HEIs!

In fact the real situation was rather more complex. First, the Jarratt Report did not adopt a wholly centralizing tendency, as some people believe. It advocated budget delegation, with accountability, and improved staff development and appraisal, including at departmental level. Second, the rhetoric of empowerment, taken up by the Quality (Total Quality Management or TQM) movement, was by no means reflected in the reality of life in every boardroom and on every shopfloor (Sherr and Teeter 1991; Bolton 1995).

So, in the absence of 'reverse polarization' between industry and academia, where do we stand now? In particular, are HEIs unsure whether to accelerate, go steady ahead or reverse in devolving control from the centre to the academic units? By their nature, HEIs have an in-built tendency towards devolution. Other organizations, some of which have prospered through central control and an all-pervading culture, are reconsidering and perhaps moving towards more local determination. For example, a report from Investors in People UK informs its assessors and providers of training about cases of companies, including Marks and Spencer, the NatWest Group and Sainsbury's, which have allowed decisions in their local branches or constituent businesses to determine whether and how they may qualify for Investors status. The report quotes as an example of radical decentralization the case of the London Borough of Brent, which in the 1980s placed 85 per cent of its staff in contractor units run as separate businesses. The change of management style has been accompanied by exceptional results: Brent's performance is now in the top third of local authorities in the UK.

Managing change

Why is it important to study the role of an academic unit – a faculty, school, department or centre – within the larger 'parent' institution? While diagnosis is necessary, it is important only because of the pressing need for change. Taking snapshots of prevailing reality is of limited value for, even in the time between the writing and the publication of this book, the environment will have changed significantly. Not all the changes are inflicted upon the sector by direct or indirect government action, as some people in HEIs believe: students, alumni, employers, journalists, commercial clients, local authorities and professional associations also contribute to pressure for change. Technological changes enable them to do so much more effectively than before and, indeed, the technology becomes a subject in itself when changes are planned.

Academic units share in the response of HEIs to the environment, but more significantly, each inhabits a unique world of its own in which it interacts directly with external, as well as internal, constituents. It might be the preferred option for some academics to analyse, reflect upon and express opinions about the nature of the changes. For those charged with managing the units – and in many respects they are *business* units – such a detached attitude is not possible. One determinant of success is the ability to anticipate or at least to capitalize upon the environment, to offer the services which the institution is well adapted to deliver to customers who, directly or indirectly, pay for those services. In short, an active approach is required from at least some members of the organization.

HEIs have been characterized as inherently conservative and risk averse by necessity. By necessity? Doesn't that contradict what has just been said about the changing environment? Institutions which have up to 70 per cent of their costs tied up in salaries and wages for staff whose contracts make them relatively difficult to redeploy or dismiss simply cannot make radical shifts in priorities: change has to be incremental. Fortunately, incremental changes which are continuous and well directed can have great impact in the medium to long term.

HEIs cannot maintain the status quo while lobbying government and various quangos for a better share of resources which, in overall terms, are shrinking. Most of them realized in the late 1970s that they required a dual strategy, one wing of which is based on the active pursuit of direct business.

Descriptions such as 'enterprising' and 'entrepreneurial' have been used to describe this approach, but those terms have acquired some political baggage in the process. Indeed language in this area tends to be unhelpfully value laden: HEIs' private sources have been called 'earned income' but this seems to insult those engaged in the very hard work of servicing the demand for teaching (and research) which is paid for largely through the funding councils. Private sources are sometimes called 'soft money' but this seems equally insulting to those who make the effort to go out and win the money in competitive, often stressful, circumstances. I prefer the term 'private' to refer to funds generated by direct approaches to the various market-places in which HEIs can operate, even though it is not yet widely used. It carries the correct connotation of distinguishing itself from 'public' funds – a term which is much better understood.

In order to achieve their purposes through generating private and public funds and to organize themselves in ways which facilitate that process, HEIs need leaders who are dispersed at many levels throughout the organization. Those leaders need to be champions of change or at least to support colleagues who are champions of change.

Change is felt even more acutely, sometimes painfully, at the level of the individual teacher whose role in the educational process is subject to so much actual, and threatened, change.

A number of factors are driving the need for change. First, consumers have become more demanding. As a result, universities are required to demonstrate how they're using resources to meet the expectations of those they serve. There is considerable concern, especially among faculty, about the legitimacy of the concept of student as customer. Whether we find this concept useful or whether we feel it threatens traditional academic values, it appears that we are being forced to acknowledge that students (and their parents) are right when they insist that they be satisfied with our product. Their satisfaction, to a considerable extent, now depends upon whether the education we provide helps them achieve their goals.

A related factor driving the need for change is the sense that universities have become insular, self-centered, and slow to change. Our mission and our performance are being evaluated in terms of the value delivered to students and the community. This has resulted in a belief that the academy's priorities are not aligned with those of its constituencies. There is no longer external support for a tradition in which we decide what students need solely on the basis of internal criteria. Instead, students feel that we need to understand their objectives and how we can contribute to the achievement of their goals . . .

If we wait until the threat is more thoroughly understood, many of the opportunities to influence the nature of the response will have been foregone. Focusing on the threat is not the most effective way to achieve a transformation; it is difficult to build a commitment to change simply on the grounds that critics don't think we know what we're doing. Rather, those involved in the organization must themselves be dissatisfied with the *status quo* and conclude that change is necessary in order for their own objectives to be achieved . . .

Achieving success over a lifetime that might include seven to ten significant career experiences imposes greater demands on the graduates of our universities. Further, today's graduates are entering a world in which they will be required to deal with uncertainty, complexity, the global village, the information explosion, other emerging technologies, and many different cultures. They must be prepared to solve problems, make decisions, and negotiate while maintaining integrity, individual stability, and social harmony. To succeed, they will need to be able to accumulate new knowledge continously and to use that knowledge spontaneously, appropriately, and in many different contexts. They will need to be able to communicate effectively and to think in a flexible and resourceful manner.

(Smith 1996: 21–2)

Thomas Gerrity recently retired as Dean of the University of Pennsylvania's Wharton School, ranked number one business school in the world every year since 1994 by *Business Week* magazine. Gerrity was founder and Chief Executive of the Index Group for 20 years before becoming Dean at Wharton.

Wharton graduates commented, 'He came from a change management background so, in some ways, he just went ahead and did what he had done in his consulting career.'

'Gerrity's fundamental insight about Wharton was that there could be a way to get different academic disciplines to work together so that Wharton graduates would develop well rounded skills and be more effective business leaders . . . Whilst Wharton had many strong individual departments, it was the teamwork among them that enabled the school to rise to the top.'

(*The Times*, 26 January 1999)

Take the illustration of an art historian who has been using a certain set of slides for his fifty-minute lectures for many years. Along comes the computer revolution, and on a CD-Rom or maybe the Internet, a student can zoom in on the eyes and nose of a portrait or whatever work of art we're talking about. How does the art historian react to that? He's scared to death. Instead of standing in front of the room showing slides, he must change his role to that of a mentor or coach, looking over his students' shoulders. It's a different role, but it's still an important one. He still has something to contribute, but he's got to be willing to change and adapt his pedagogy to technology and its impact on students' learning styles. That can be very scary.

   I think colleges and universities have been a bit unfair about all of this, because they have not been willing to put the resources into what used to be called faculty development or redevelopment or retraining. If you expect someone to play a different role, you've got to give that person an opportunity to adapt to that new role, and you've also got to provide some training. It isn't fair just to announce, 'Change!'

(Graduate Management
Admissions Council 1997: 33)

Hence we rapidly reach issues in training and development which are examined more fully in Chapter 10.

2

DECISION MAKING

The unit may be compact so that communication can be direct and personal. Contiguous offices and open doors may facilitate consultation and a sense of involvement. Unfortunately, such a model was probably applicable only to small and medium sized departments in the days before resources per student began to nose dive and before research came to be so rigorously assessed.

This scenario is not being raised in order to be dismissed as a piece of nostalgia. The traditional collegial model, readily implanted into the new universities of the mid-1960s, still exists as an ideal. It exists as a reality in better resourced pockets of the sector. However, those pockets are now less likely to be autonomous units; the policies and decisions which emanate from collegial roots are now more likely to flow into a larger decision-making unit – typically a faculty rather than a department. As such those policies and decisions may not carry sway; they may be diluted or contradicted by other groupings or by a dictate from on high. None the less it is important for morale that collegial processes should be retained wherever possible. We all feel better having voted for the losing faction than having been denied a vote.

Burton Clark's book on entrepreneurial universities in Europe, *Creating Entrepreneurial Universities: Organizational Pathways of Transformation* (International Association of Universities/Elsevier Science, 1998) shows that there is no necessary contradiction between collegial attitudes and entrepreneurial behaviour, albeit one suspects that some members of the collegium tend to become spectators when business matters are thrashed out.

'Successful entrepreneurialism requires collegial attitudes and forms. Enterprising universities simplify their structure radically: they locate central authority in one operational committee, or in a small set of interlocked committees; they greatly increase the competence of central administrative staff; they bring better management into the underlying structure of faculties, departments and research centres. But collegial integration is maintained, even increased, by bringing faculty into the central bodies, often in dominating numbers, and insisting on faculty–administration integration all along the line. The entrepreneurialism of groups dominates individual entrepreneurship. Effective transformation rests upon collegial entrepreneurialism. Hard managerialism is a road not taken – or not for very long.

A well-worked-out entrepreneurial style unhooks collegiality from defence of the *status quo* and the love of the *status quo ante*. It becomes biased in favour of adaptiveness and change. The installation of a spirit of collegial entrepreneurialism takes a bit of doing, perhaps even ten to 15 years of hard work, but the outcome is priceless.

As more universities work out new patterns of finance and organization, learning by experimentation becomes an ever more important maxim. It applies from one department to another, among universities within a national system and among universities thrown into an international orbit. The wisdom of those who have worked out a successful transformation can be highly instructive.

The culture of higher education can absorb the risks of entrepreneurship. Fund-raising from other than traditional mainline patrons need not be squalid. Old hard monies have turned soft; institutions can sit for a very long time, rather like Estragon and Vladimir, waiting for ministers "to come to their senses" and send more money. Part and parcel of the entrepreneurial response is the clear-headed recognition that dependable returns come with a diversified portfolio of supporters and income streams. Not any income channels, however, only those that befit the fundamental values of a university.'

Burton R. Clark, emeritus professor at the graduate school of education, University of California Los Angeles.

(*The Times Higher*, 22 May 1998)

Wise managers think of ways of harnessing collegial processes. For example, it may not be possible to determine budgets or student intake targets by consensus, but other important decisions, such as on reward systems or on facilities to be provided to staff or students, can be informed by consultation. Managers of systems should also be aware that the onus is upon them every time they choose to override collegial methods of decision making. If 'they' decide to make a central decision rather than to consult those interested in the outcome, then that decision should be well researched, well considered and effectively implemented. Few things cause greater widespread cynicism than a perception that the institution is being led by people who not only have little interest in involving staff in decisions, but also manage those decisions incompetently.

Within a unit there should be scope for collegial activity. At minimum, this could be a departmental meeting or forum which provides a news-giving function. Ideally it is the opportunity also for bottom-up ideas to be circulated. Generating ideas is a distinctive strength of academics, so why not use it? An embattled dean will probably otherwise have very little leisure to rethink strategy or snatch a passing opportunity. The meeting/forum can also be given formal powers in the event of an emergency. It is reassuring for members of a faculty to know that, in an extreme scenario in which corruption or incompetence arose and could not be cured by management action, they could throw a democratic switch by calling an extraordinary meeting and conveying a message to the chief executive of the institution or even beyond the institution. Wise rule-makers would ensure that an emergency could not simply be declared by a maverick individual or pressure group: no meeting would be called unless a specified and substantial percentage of the staff concerned wished it.

Leaders should find that using the collegium wherever it can be effective is well worth the inevitable delay, use of precious time and reiteration of arguments. They cannot expect that a consensus will actually be the result and if they allow proposals to be shelved until such time as a consensus arises, they will wait a long time. Their leadership will become paralysed. Courage to proceed, in the face of widespread scepticism or of vocal opposition from a few, is the mark of a leader. Having heard and contributed to the arguments, the leader or leading group may decide that it is their duty to opt for the idea which is ahead of its time. These tend to be defining moments in a period of academic leadership. With hindsight we will know whether they showed superior wisdom and courage, or wilful behaviour based on poor judgement.

Inability to generate a consensus, other than in exceptional circumstances, is only one limitation of the collegium. Such groupings have proved inadequate for decision making in several ways. Academic jealousies are often directed most fiercely to those in cognate departments so that, ironically, the faculty is ineffective because several of its constituent departments would prefer 'equal misery' to the prospect of funding being directed selectively according to some merit-based system. Sometimes these jealousies are deeply based on personal views of the world. Staff concerned may know nothing about other faculties, but enough about the department along the corridor to form a caricature of it and lobby against it. Such situations are exploited by the rest of the institution: by other faculties which can be coherent and work collaboratively, and by central officers and committees which can readily pursue a divide-and-rule policy.

A further weakness of the collegium emerges when it pronounces on practical matters. Unless they accept the advice of an academic directorate or manager, collegial bodies are capable of curious decisions. Each group or department may have its own rules on charging students for photocopies of articles, or on penalties for late submission of coursework. The suggestion that the differences should be discussed, then eliminated by adopting a standard set of measures, may be rejected as managerialist and dictatorial. Members of the group are unaware that to students in several departments housed in the same building, the differences are inexplicable, unfair, foolish, irritating. Again, if not willing to take advice on implementation, collegial bodies can take decisions which simply cannot be made to stick or which fall to no one to manage and monitor.

Collegial bodies often operate effectively when acting as a talking shop – because talking shops can be valuable in academia. It is normally not a good idea to graft on to them decision-making functions which require a different mind-set. Nor is it likely that the unit will be sufficiently well resourced to afford the services of an administrator to prepare briefing papers and to record anything more than skeletal notes of discussion and decisions for such bodies.

Decision-making bodies within the academic unit are likely to include at least one of five kinds: a faculty board or board of studies, a policy and resources committee (PRC), a senior management group (SMG), an advisory board, and subcommittees and other bodies.

Faculty board or board of studies

The faculty board or board of studies is normally a formal body of the HEI. It tends to comprise either all members of academic staff in the unit, and perhaps some from other parts of the HEI and student representatives, or representatives from each department within the faculty. The chief function of the board is to approve academic proposals, typically new courses or amendments to existing courses. It is the expert body without whose approval proposals cannot proceed from their originators to the Senate, which is the chief academic body. The board is perhaps the main academic watchdog, the guardian of standards, certainly a major component of the institution's quality assurance process. At higher levels, academic proposals are unlikely to receive rigorous consideration because members do not possess sufficient knowledge of the subject. Those higher bodies generally confine themselves to ensuring that matters such as contact hours and assessment are consistent with institutional policy and with comparable courses, and that changes seem strategically appropriate in that they complement rather than compete with existing programmes.

The boards do not always provide the informed, collegial atmosphere which should ideally be a feature of an academically lively institution. They meet only once or twice a term, a feature which, when combined with frequent changes in membership or low levels of attendance, tends to mean that a shared sense of purpose rarely develops. Managers of business items and those proposing changes tend to put pressure on the board to approve the proposals with minimum changes. This is the case because there is often urgency about gaining approval so that a new teaching programme may be advertised and launched by a particular date. If a proposal is referred back for further consideration, three or four months may be lost before it can resume its place on the ladder of approval.

Some members are seen at board meetings only when they have an item to propose. Some attend only out of a sense of departmental duty, to help ensure that their colleagues' proposal is approved. Others steadfastly decline to comment on proposals from other departments, perhaps deferring to their superior knowledge of the subject or, equally likely, implementing a live-and-let-live policy: they do not speak against others' proposals on the understanding that the same courtesy will be extended to them on another occasion. A few members relish making mischief by repeatedly raising objections to any proposals from one or more other departments or, in some cases, from their own colleagues. Members who take an active and constructive part in discussion with the interest of the faculty as a whole at heart are seldom seen. Fortunately, some of them end up as chair of the board or of important working groups.

'Live-and-let-live' is not the civilized, collegial situation it may appear. It lends itself to a lowering of standards as members suppress legitimate concerns about what is going on elsewhere in the faculty. They turn a blind eye to actions which may be sloppy, inappropriate or needlessly at variance with established good practice. This is an example of academics failing to exercise corporate responsibility, and of mutual back-scratching under the guise of academic freedom.

Most boards have the power to discuss matters of policy and, indeed, almost any matter may land on the agenda, either top-down on a reference from Senate or a management group or bottom-up at the request of a member. In that respect the boards can perform a valuable function, albeit members can be frustrated by the fact that the board is unlikely to have executive control over anything other than course approval.

Policy and resources committee

Policy (or planning) and resources committees became fashionable in the wake of the Jarratt Report (1985). They tend to comprise heads of department, subject groups or course leaders who are the chief actors in the management of a faculty. They tend to operate like a cabinet, to concentrate on questions of strategy and choices about resources. They are normally chaired by a dean but the expectations of the group will tend to determine the dean's role. At one end of the spectrum, the dean is the leader of the faculty and chiefly responsible for the appointment of the heads who form the rest of the committee. The dean may use the body not only as a sounding board but also as a means of line management and top-down communications. The committee would not be expected to challenge or vary the decisions of the dean and senior management group until the time comes for the appointment of the dean to be reviewed.

At the other end of the spectrum, the committee is a gathering of territorially minded heads who perforce have to cooperate with one another in order that the unit can run. The dean's function as chair is often just that – to chair meetings and to avoid the imbalance which could result from one of the heads acting as chair. The dean then represents the committee in central bodies but on this model behaves more like an elected representative rather than a leader. The institution may find it convenient to deal with one representative rather than six or seven separate heads, but it must know that the dean's ability to make a long-term commitment or to make decisions stick is strictly limited by a relatively unempowered position back at base.

Some institutions have acted equivocally by nominating deans as line managers of substantial academic groups without giving them sufficient constitutional power: it may simply be too easy for a head of department to defy or ignore a decision of the dean or the PRC. The centre may accept the benefits of rationalization, happily using the deans' offices to gather and circulate information rather than interfacing with every separate department or group. At the same time they may deny effective power to the deans by concentrating control in the hands of the vice-chancellor, pro-vice-chancellors and whoever else forms the institution's senior management group. Deans need and deserve to know that they will receive backing from above if they are challenged from below.

The PRC is likely to meet more often than the board and, also by means of its smaller numbers, be more capable of taking business decisions. Business tends to be initiated by the dean or associate deans or in response to the requirements of the institution centrally, although there is no reason why ideas and proposals should not originate from the constituent departments. The PRC performs a range of functions, from ensuring that the actions of the dean are open to scrutiny, to tactical matters such as who will say what at the next meeting of Senate. The committee also has an important function for communications, linking the individual members of faculty with the unit's executive body. However, for this to be effective, the head of department has to act as intermediary. There is a risk that, when at PRC, heads will represent their personal views rather than those of their colleagues. Also they may omit to convey from PRC to their colleagues items of news and impressions relevant to the department. It can be frustrating for a dean to discover that, whereas some heads have not broadcast important pieces of information, they have nevertheless divulged confidential information gleaned from PRC.

To be more positive, there are undoubted benefits in the use of a PRC to govern an academic unit. When the inevitable problems arise, they can be shared and solved in a positive manner. Department A seems unable to balance its books, department B is reliably believed to have pulled down the unit's average score in the RAE, department C is experiencing difficulty in attracting sufficient students, department D has lost several key staff and apparently cannot attract replacements of adequate calibre. In the 'spokes-of-the-wheel' model, each department would face an investigation from a central body and this could prove to be an unsympathetic, ineffective, potentially damaging or punitive experience. Under the faculty system, the dean can assure the central bodies that he or she is taking responsibility for solving the problem. This is made sustainable if the 'bottom line' for the faculty is healthy. A chronic deficit in one department within a surplus-generating faculty is not likely to head a busy finance officer's worry list.

Does this mean that the problem will be under the carpet instead of those responsible being on the carpet? Far from it. The rest of faculty will recognize that it is endangered by a weakness in its own area and it will be more likely to discover solutions than a less well informed external group. Above all, the departments with the problem will be unable to hide at their own PRC. Bluster and denial are not an option in one's own academic backyard. If the committee is functioning effectively, the rest will neither gloat nor condemn. On other issues, they could be the weak link and so are encouraged to hear and understand the problem and contribute to its solution.

The faculty PRC is unfortunately also prey to weaknesses inherent in many academic committees. Imagining themselves to be uninvolved or being deferential can lead members to acquiesce in decisions driven by an energetic deanery. Years later the PRC may repent its silent approval for a scheme to validate a programme taught by a college in the Middle East. Inactivity can be destructive in other ways. Heads may cease to care for their own departmental destiny, confident that the faculty is now the active operational unit. The dean is seen as the protector and the focus for all initiatives but these initiatives become hampered by lack of input from departments who expect to be told where to divert their resources. The unit runs out of champions and an insufficiently critical eye is cast over proposals.

All this presupposes that the PRC gets to first base as an operational unit. This can happen only if the heads put aside their right to behave as turf guardians and to treat every decision as a negotiation from which they must wring maximum advantage. Somehow a sense of shared purpose and, preferably, a degree of mutual respect has to exist or be generated before the PRC can become effective.

Just as problems have to be shared throughout the unit, so should successes. Faculties which are merely a loose confederation for administrative convenience will not reflect back and capitalize upon the successes of one department, group or individual. If one or two departments report successes in these circumstances, the faculty scarcely benefits; indeed it may be perceived to suffer because non-achievement elsewhere in the faculty may stand out by contrast. Managing perceptions or, if you wish, spin-doctoring, can raise the profile of the whole faculty within and beyond the institution.

Good management in general, not just good management of information, can also promote the unit. A convincing case that progress is planned and evaluated on a collective basis can create a glow effect which enhances perceptions of the whole activity. It is only human to be influenced by good presentation when assessing control processes, quality of teaching, even quality of research.

Senior management group

The senior management group is used as a steering committee for the PRC, preparing its agenda and acting on its behalf when immediate action is necessary. Typically meeting once a week, the group may operate informally, perhaps with only skeletal minutes. It can be extremely powerful, concentrating in one place the dean, associate deans and faculty administrator. Unless a deliberate effort is made to include one or two elected representatives, the group may take major decisions in short order without consultation. With the benefit of advice from his or her closest counsellors, the dean will be less inhibited in taking decisions than when acting alone. The SMG has the strength of regularly ensuring that momentum is maintained and efforts concentrated and, as long as the PRC and board are properly consulted, those actions will be within agreed policy. Unless something has gone wrong with the group dynamics, the atmosphere of SMG meetings will be mutually supportive and freed from the need to pay homage to departmental boundaries. The danger is of another kind – that an uncritical 'group-think' may set in. Associate deans, possibly the appointees of the dean, may tell the dean only what he or she wishes to hear and all may become part of an unconscious conspiracy to disregard evidence which may contradict the 'party line'.

Just as at central institutional level, there is a risk that the faculty's SMG may pay little heed to others whose opinions it may dismiss as predictable, narrowly self-interested or simply uninformed and naive. If operating largely through a SMG with an ineffective PRC or board, the dean would do well to find ways of listening to advice from elsewhere such as from junior staff or external people with an interest in the faculty.

Advisory board

Faculties or schools with substantial external interests have formed an advisory board with a range of objectives, including the following:

- to seek ways to influence a selected set of influential external people who may be in a position to promote the interests of the faculty, possibly including fund-raising;
- to seek advice and comment from leading practitioners on the strategies and priorities of the faculty;
- to strengthen the unit's hand in internal bargaining processes by fielding a group of people capable of influencing central bodies and senior officers;
- to form contacts which help students to obtain work experience placements and employment after graduation;
- to demonstrate the practical relevance of the faculty's work;

- to honour practitioners through association with senior academics, particularly in cases where the practitioners themselves have had little formal academic training;
- to provide practitioners with the opportunity to network with one another.

If some of these objectives seem valuable and attainable, it is worth considering the establishment of an advisory board. At the outset, important choices have to be made. For example, is it preferable to form a large body of people with time to spare – in which case many of them will be retired – or a small body of practitioners who are actively engaged in business? The former choice may provide wisdom and engagement but little in the way of fresh ideas and influence, whereas the latter choice may give access to a cutting-edge of up-to-date ideas and contacts but with a risk that members will have other priorities and miss more meetings than they can attend.

In either case it is wise to arm oneself with a formal procedure which enables the faculty to drop inactive or interfering members without offence at the end of their term of office.

Some deans are wary of advisory boards, particularly if members donate funds, then expect to exercise control over the uses of the gift. There is also a risk that members will bring an unsophisticated approach to the faculty's problems which they imagine can be solved by well-judged sackings and table-thumping. The first problem is in the category 'nice to have' and not a reality in most institutions while the second can be contained by demonstrating the complexity of institutional politics. It is best to steer an advisory board clear of internal minefields such as budget negotiations or personnel practice.

Deans should be keen to engage with the outside world in promoting the interests of their unit: being able to manage and make the most of those who are willing to help is an important diplomatic skill. Members of boards wish to have something valuable to do, rather than to listen to long reports on work within the faculty. Why not set them up to research on matters such as lobbying politicians, relations with the media, advertising campaigns, publication of brochures, identifying prospective customers, maximizing income or benchmarking studies of rival institutions? Then be prepared to involve them in the implementation of the recommendations they bring back.

Without giving the advisory board executive powers, it is worth rehearsing regular decisions within that forum. It helps the board to appreciate the difficult world you inhabit and occasionally a member may come up with a valuable insight. Sometimes it takes an outsider to spot the blindingly obvious.

Subcommittees and other bodies ∎

The PRC may choose to free itself from minutiae by setting up sub-committees which can draw on expert opinion and act on its behalf. Whether it is important that the subcommittees too should fully represent every significant operational unit within the faculty is a matter for judgement. Subjects which might merit a subcommittee include teaching, research, finance, information technology (IT) and facilities such as laboratories, lecture rooms and minor works. Some of these are practically indispensable: a teaching committee of experienced academics to form one of several layers within the quality assurance process is essential and it is also essential that it is provided with high-calibre administrative support. A unit with strong research needs a forum to discuss its priorities, whether that is selecting and bidding for major grants and contracts or coordinating the work of lone scholars into mutually supportive research groups. In the other areas listed above, the unit may find it beneficial to bring proposals to a formal committee, if only to demonstrate fair treatment in the carving up of financial allocations. However, it should be aware of the dangers of letting committees loose into areas which are someone's management responsibility. Committees are notoriously bad at making effective operational decisions, particularly where the chair seeks to achieve consensus. Why make someone responsible for monitoring budgets, for buying software or for refurbishing laboratories, then hedge that person round with committees which may contain people with an axe to grind and without any responsibility? Officers responsible should be told to use their judgement and should be accountable. They might be expected to consult before arriving at decisions.

Servicing committees provides an insight into how some academic institutions have proved so ineffective at managing themselves.

Principles of the committee structure

There are four main principles of the committee structure:

1 *Effectiveness*: decisions should be wise, legal, authoritative and accountable.
2 *Efficiency*: the system should use the least possible resources of time, money and energy.
3 *Representativeness*: it is important to promote transparency of process and involvement of members of the university.
4 *Accountability*: accountability could be taken much further: members should be accountable for their actions as members of a

committee and, if also representing an interest group, accountable to that interest group. Instances of adequate briefing and debriefing between representatives of faculties/departments and their colleagues seem rare and, in so far as such processes are inadequate, potential benefits of the committee system (genuine representativeness and good communications) are not being achieved.

No doubt there will be many bodies on which representatives will continue to be required. However, I believe that personal qualities should be weighted more heavily when membership is planned. These might be *competence, experience* and *commitment*. Those qualities, diverted towards a more active system ('working groups' or 'task forces' rather than committees as we currently know them) would tend to produce the more effective and accountable outcomes which we desire.

The number of management and operational committees should be reduced. The officers concerned should be accountable as part of a management structure and should not be constrained by committees of this kind. If it is thought that such a system cannot be employed at this university, then the question should be asked: why is this so?

(From my personal submission to
a review of a committee structure)

Challenging obstacles to change in a
semi-autonomous unit

The question is how to introduce a 'culture of change' in order to 'change the culture' within a semi-autonomous unit. The unit runs a devolved budget and the centre of the institution uses a hands-off approach to academic matters in general while offering guidelines. Normally units welcome this approach because it gives the ability to manage their own affairs including in the areas of assessment, quality, appeals and academic management in general. But what happens in the case of a school that achieved an 'excellent' when last subjected to a Teaching Quality Assessment (TQA) visit, has an abhorrence of bureaucratic requirements and believes that everything it does is fine? The centre has general guidelines and recommendations which it invites schools to implement; this is used as a reason for not changing as they are recommendations and not requirements.

There are two approaches to overcoming opposition to change: the direct and the indirect approach. The direct approach relies on submitting proposals to the unit's academic board, and hoping that those who attend pass the resolutions without too many queries, and that the implementation will follow because the board says so.

The indirect approach is to target some key players – course director or head of department – and convince them that not only is change required, but also it is actually their idea. This then builds a momentum for change, the culture is slowly 'manipulated' and when proposals are introduced, acceptance and implementation follow with support from these key faculty. By following the indirect approach, it is also possible to influence the central administration and achieve change there as well.

3

ALLOCATING RESOURCES

Delivery with scarce resources

Whatever system of resource allocation is in place, the activities and atmosphere of the academic unit are largely the product of choices made by the unit itself. How non-payroll expenditure is budgeted, actioned and monitored is likely to be less influential than choices about use of time. What skills have been identified as priorities and hence guided the recruitment of staff? Which activities are disregarded or compressed into minimum amounts of time in order to release maximum time for which other activities? Most units are experiencing changes which have caused them to think about, and act upon, such questions more frequently than they did in the past.

When planning the allocation of resources at university or faculty level, the notion of a matrix can be helpful. Along one axis are *resources*, the most important of which are academic staff; along the other axis are *activities*, major ones being teaching programmes and research.

In a simple faculty structure, nothing beyond an aggregation of department-based matrices is required. There are no significant external calls on a department's resources. However, if the faculty is committed to activities on a multidepartmental basis, competing claims will arise. Some staff will be expected to take part in multidisciplinary research projects, others to teach on generalist programmes. What happens if a department, having completed its matrix, declares that it is 'full', all available resources being required for the department's own teaching and research programmes? Is it acceptable for them to contribute nothing to the faculty's other work? If so, would it still be acceptable if the staff were delivering a loss-making MSc programme with an average student to staff ratio of eight to one? Or if the time allowance for research were double the average for the faculty? When such uncomfortable questions arise, it becomes clear where power really lies. It is certainly dangerous for a faculty to commit itself to a high volume of multidepartmental activities without having first claim on staff resources or at least a guaranteed share of them. The dean may not have the *right* to call upon resources, let alone named individuals, unless a department is dedicated to the work concerned. However, in a faculty committed to the collective achievement of goals, refusal would not be expected.

Workload models

The management of staff workloads is important if there is to be a sense of equity within the faculty. For reasons of size and complexity, it may be appropriate to handle the allocation of staff resources at department or subject group level rather than expect the dean or an associate dean to mastermind the task. There will also be a benefit in terms of ownership if much of the exercise is carried out locally. However, to preserve a sense of equity, variations in norms from department to department should be minimized. A prime task for a PRC should be to decide the acceptable range of local variation. An hour's lecture might count as three hours in the allocation system, to include time required for preparation and revision of material whereas an hour's tutorial might count for two hours. However, inexperienced members of staff on probation should be given every opportunity to establish themselves as active researchers; someone developing a new course should ideally be given an enhanced time allowance to enable the background work to be carried out; an administrative role such as postgraduate admissions should carry a time allowance appropriate to the marketing effort and size of intake concerned; a confirmed non-researcher should expect to receive an allowance of time for scholarship, keeping up with the subject, but not for original research, and hence a heavier than average load of teaching and administration. Allowances must reflect what the faculty can afford: in one institution, an average of eight contact hours a week might look like a tough assignment whereas in another it might seem impossibly generous.

How do you measure the cake which is to be sliced up? Individuals' commitment and capacity are almost certain to vary so you have to define a working year, even if everyone actually works more or fewer hours. After deducting weekends, statutory and customary holidays and five weeks' holiday, even though length of holiday is not always defined in academic staff contracts, there are actually

220, not 365, days in a year. If there is an average of 7.3 hours in a working day, we can calculate that for each member of staff there are 1600 hours available for allocation. Disputes will always arise about the accuracy of each time allocation as the time spent reflects the commitment and level of competence of the individual. Clearly the system cannot be seen to reward incompetence or the devotion of extra hours to activities for which income is strictly limited or shrinking. However, if the allowances are too tough, then staff will be forced either to drive themselves into excessive stress and burnout or to cut corners and so jeopardize the quality of what is produced. Allowances should reflect the time required by a 'reasonably competent' person. The head of department has to be the interpreter of this concept. The individual, too, has choices remaining. Lecturers may choose to spend more time than their allowance on teaching and administration and put in correspondingly less time on research. No immediate mechanism is likely to check this but the time will come when they have to account for the quality and quantity of publications which they can submit to the next RAE. If the lecturer is judged to be underperforming on research then pressure will be exerted – either to make better use of research time or to become more productive in other respects.

Some units, such as the business schools at the universities of Aston and Loughborough, have evolved relatively sophisticated models for allocating work to academic staff. The key word is 'evolved': both Aston and Loughborough have refined their model over ten years. There are many pitfalls awaiting anyone who intends to introduce a right-first-time system, particularly since organizational complexities (themselves subject to constant change) and personal sensitivities are foremost.

Aston's system translates effort by staff into full-time equivalent (FTE) student numbers generated by it. The advantage of this system is that it measures outputs rather than inputs; the outputs are then connected with the various levels of income accompanying various categories of FTE student. Each school can choose weightings which reflect its own priorities and provide incentives for staff to pursue activities commensurate with those priorities. For example, if the unit's aim is to increase the number of doctoral students and to improve the quality of supervision given to them, it could increase the number of points allocated to the activity.

Loughborough uses a model based upon staff hours. A target number of teaching hours is assigned to each individual member of staff in preference to the use of student FTEs on the grounds that assigning weights, for example as between lectures and tutorials, or allowances for marking, tends to be an arbitrary process exacerbated by the fact that student registrations may be unknown until after a course begins, making forecasting and planning too difficult. The Loughborough model has been adjusted to reflect a growing desire to emphasize research. It does so subtly by allocating points for 'primary' (refereed academic journals) publications and 'secondary' publications, then finding each individual's highest average score in each of the past four years. Staff also assess their own research rating and may make a case based on forthcoming publications before their rating is decided. Despite the undoubted benefits of an objective system of this kind, there are dangers to morale if ratings, particularly for research, become public and are used to classify and label individuals.

Benefits of load allocation systems include the following:

- Improved fairness and transparency make it easier for heads to be seen to give equitable treatment and for perceptions of unfairness to be challenged.
- There is an in-built cross-check that the total amount of work to be done balances the amount of resource available to do it. A total load for the unit emerges from, or originates, the sum of individuals' loads.
- Cases for additional resources at the level of the unit can be readily assessed and supported by evidence. Units with more resource than allocated load would be expected either to do more work on behalf of others or to reduce expenditure.
- If activities are scored appropriately, staff have incentives to cut back on activities which generate relatively low amounts of FTE student load and income. However, this tendency has to be monitored in case it encourages staff to short-change their students.
- The model can be revised at any time to reflect changed priorities and circumstances.

Disadvantages of load models include the following:

- There is an excessive amount of data collection for administrators. The evidence is that the burden is acceptable if the work is concentrated at a particular point in the year according to agreed norms.
- There is an undue focus on earning points. Even if some points are available for 'citizenship', they will be heavily outweighed by allocations for teaching and research, hence making it harder to get volunteers for duties which carry no or few points.
- There are no magic solutions. Some individuals who have unique skills or, conversely, can offer less than other colleagues, will still have their duties assigned, even if they have to carry an overload or underload until staffing solutions can be found.

- Staff may nitpick their allocations, arguing for extra points. Flexibility should be built in to accommodate good arguments, but Loughborough hit upon the idea of having scores increase exponentially (2, 4, 8, 16, 32, 64). Lobbying for incremental change is not permitted: to win the argument that the activity is incorrectly scored, one would have to demonstrate that its points score should be at least doubled.

The balance seems to fall clearly in favour of running a load model. Staff tend to argue about scores for individual activities but do not question the validity of the process, once established. However, it is important that the measures should be transparent, owned and open to appeal. The usefulness of doing so is clear: not only do people feel that their opinion has been heard but also, in doing so, they contribute to a healthy debate about the unit's strategy and priorities. They also see clearly how their work contributes to the unit's overall effort and output.

For a full discussion of the issues surrounding the use of load models, see Finlay and Gregory (1994), King and Pile (1997) and Higson *et al.* (1998).

Matching resource allocation with strategy

Every unit, except the smallest and most simple, runs multiple activities each of which should be capable of analysis so that cost-effectiveness can be measured. The worst outcome is ignorance so that one does not know whether a downturn in one activity and an increase in another would leave the unit stronger or weaker financially.

For analysis to be possible, set out to identify the level of income associated with each activity and relate that to the effort required to resource it. The concept of staff loads explored above will be needed in order to determine that the department's MSc programme which has 18 students absorbs the equivalent of, say, two members of academic staff and half of a secretary. Its undergraduate units may enrol the equivalent of 250 students and absorb five members of academic staff and one secretary. Having calculated the respective level of funding generated by the students and done some arithmetic may not lead to the conclusion that the department should abandon its postgraduate provision. For example, it may not be possible to expand the undergraduate work and there may be no realistic other sources of income apart from the postgraduate programme. However, if the department is forgoing opportunities to generate more funding from research, or from other teaching which may bring more income per student, then the question of withdrawal from the post-graduate programme becomes more pointed.

Overall, it will be necessary for the activities to generate a surplus of income over expenditure in order to cover indirect costs and overheads. These include items such as staffing to run the office, telephones, stationery, postage, printing, advertising, hospitality, travel, equipment, maintenance, staff development and, in some institutions, accommodation. Some of these items are 'general' and cannot be attributed other than arbitrarily to activities. The unit may either regard them as general expenses and cover them from the surplus on activities or charge them, however crudely, to those activities. At the next level of aggregation, a school or faculty will deal with the income streams and expenditure of constituent departments and of multidepartmental activities. For example, a faculty of science may include three departments and a degree course in combined science which is a faculty responsibility.

For a faculty, balancing the books is not simply a matter of taking a few more students here and cutting down on travel costs there.

The decline in government funding means that the unit of resource is not able to sustain the quality of teaching and learning environment to which many HEIs aspire. There are increasingly challenging savings targets and requirements to cross-subsidize teaching from other, private income streams, such as full-cost students, research and consultancy, and intellectual property rights. The price of financial dependence has been an erosion of autonomy from government advice, leading to greater rigidity of institutional structures. The community and the economy, however, prefer relevance and a rich diversity of differentiated models. This greater market segmentation suggests that HEIs must be imaginative and innovative in their structures and that management practices must be tailored to fit specific circumstances.

A good resource allocation formula reflects and reinforces strategy. The common element should be to attain stable, continuous and diverse resourcing, a substantial element of which remains the recurrent grant. The funding councils' resource allocation formulae are highly visible, but HEIs would be negligent in their duty to manage their resources if they simply mimicked them. However, common aims by the funding council, institution and faculty to provide high-quality education, to enhance the quality of research and to ensure staff satisfaction can result in different resource strategies. Different formulae reflect different strategies, but departments must reconcile them and be accountable for the use of those resources. Therefore, balance of payments should be only one of the factors taken into account in making strategic decisions.

Table 3.1 A faculty's first draft budget (all figures in £k)

	General	Dept A	Dept B	Dept C	Masters	Total
Income						
Funding council tuition		400	600	300	400	1700
Tuition		200	300	150	200	850
Full-cost (private) tuition		500	100	50	500	1150
Funding council research	1300					1300
Private research		50	100			150
Total	1300	1150	1100	500	1100	5150
Expenditure						
Academic staff payroll	70	650	650	430		1800
Support staff payroll	50	40	50	40	40	220
Non-payroll	30	260	200	70	150	710
Total	150	950	900	540	190	2730
Surplus (Deficit)	1150	200	200	(40)	910	2420

A faculty with three departments and a multidisciplinary Masters programme might present a first draft budget such as the one shown in Table 3.1.

Department A has 13 academic staff. It is difficult to recruit suitable members of faculty so salaries have been driven beyond the average for the sector. It has an excellent international reputation and attracts large numbers of postgraduate students, who pay premium fees. Department B has 17 academic staff and a heavy reliance on public-funded teaching. Department C has 10 academic staff and has experienced difficulties in recruiting students. It has few other sources of income and relatively high fixed costs.

At the next stage, the faculty must decide how it will apportion

- a contribution of £2,369,000 to the rest of the institution;
- the income of £1,300,000 from the funding councils in respect of the RAE-based rating of its research;
- the teaching required to resource the large Masters programme.

The institution is asking the faculty to contribute 46 per cent of its income to cover central institutional costs and to cross-subsidize two other faculties which are certain to be in deficit. This will leave a budget surplus of £51,000, which is approximately 1 per cent of the faculty's total income.

The faculty will make a judgement about the research funding. If its allocation reflected the known performance of individual staff, it

Table 3.2 A faculty's second draft budget

	General	Dept A	Dept B	Dept C	Masters	Total
Income		1150	1100	500	1100	5150
Research allocation		705	460	135		1300
Revised total		1855	1560	635	1100	5150
Expenditure						
Direct	150	950	900	540	190	2730
Contribution	130	824	781	469	165	2369
Revised total	280	1774	1681	1009	355	5099
Surplus (Deficit)	(280)	81	(121)	(374)	745	51

Table 3.3 A faculty's final position

	General	Dept A	Dept B	Dept C	Masters	Total
Previous surplus (Deficit)	(280)	81	(121)	(374)	745	51
Net transfers for Masters programme	0	190	170	240	(600)	0
Bought-in teaching		(51)				(51)
Final	(280)	220	49	(134)	145	0

would give proportionately most to department A and least to department C. Having already decided to share the central institutional charge *pro rata* to total expenditure, it would produce an allocation such as the one in Table 3.2.

The income-generating units fund the cost of the faculty office. The departments are also required to share the teaching of the Masters programme, in exchange for which the programme makes cash transfers to the teaching departments. In an ideal world the relatively underworked department C will pick up much of the load and so bring itself into balance. However, it may be that some of the material from C is not suitable for the programme, which requires substantial teaching contributions from the overstretched department A. Until a strategic rethink can take place, the faculty may have to face the possibility that even after transfer payments have been made, department C will remain in deficit on the year, department B will work hard and earn enough to put itself in surplus and department A will insist that it can meet the demand for its teaching only by buying in external teaching. The cost of that teaching – £51,000 – will put the faculty at a break-even position. Its desire to generate a surplus in order to invest in its future is put on hold for another year.

The final position is shown in Table 3.3.

4

SETTING STRATEGY

Exploring choices

Starting from scratch is a luxury very few academic leaders have experienced. Normally, their choices are constrained by a mixed inheritance. Staff cannot simply be removed or redirected or re-energized; established procedures take time to be streamlined or abolished; extra income cannot suddenly be switched on; a culture of complacency or inertia cannot quickly become energetic.

Incoming leaders should spend time listening and forming a considered view of strengths, weaknesses and possibilities before being tempted to meet expectations by taking decisive actions. Those early decisions, based on imperfect first impressions or on what others have stated as their impression of the unit, can prove disastrous in that they can permanently alienate groups and individuals whose support may be vital to the success of the enterprise. Research (Bensimon 1993; Neumann 1990) shows that making mistakes is more likely early on, particularly since the error may be contained in the process followed, as well as in the choice itself. Time spent in consultation may pay off: those who feel they have not been consulted are far more likely to oppose or fail to support the leader's choice.

The unit is unlikely to be already set up to achieve the next set of objectives laid down in its strategy. There may not be the staff to teach the desired programme or the means to attract the students. Assuming there is such a gap, the unit should look first within itself to assess how it could improve its situation. Alongside that process the unit should keep open communications with the centre of the institution. Can the centre add to the unit's views on how to enable the extra professor to be hired, the students to be recruited, the quality of the learning environment to be enhanced?

You may believe that you can double the unit's income from postgraduate programmes by a combination of increasing student numbers and fees charged. However, you may have to spend in order to generate the income. You feel that a virtuous cycle is almost within your reach. A combination of new recruitment and intensive staff development can create a high-quality teaching team in a high-demand subject; the higher fees will enable you to spend time on the students and project the message that the programme is top class; the students will gain great added value from the experience and capture attractive jobs; the programme's reputation will advance further as a result. You can see a rising curve of extra income, from £20,000 in year 1 to £500,000 in year 5 of the expansion.

An institution worth its salt will expect each unit to define a strategy. If you are fortunate, it will allow considerable degrees of freedom within it such that, for example, one unit may develop a distinctive and predominantly regional identity, perhaps drawing secondary, tertiary and further education colleges into an integrated model of provision, collaborating closely with comparable units in other HEIs in the region. Another unit might define itself on an international scale, seeking out collaboration with leading researchers in continental Europe or the US, aiming to recruit a majority of international students, setting up international exchanges and placements, and recruiting international staff.

Some institutions are not comfortable with such a diverse portfolio. It could prove difficult to govern an HEI comprising units with markedly different priorities: the institution could be little more than a holding company for a set of self-determining subsidiaries. However, if each unit is successful in its pursuit of excellence, different emphases may not be a problem. It would be more damaging for the institution if it were to define a particular mission for all, but find that it was markedly more successful in some units than in others. Pluralism is almost a natural state for a university and as institutions have grown in size, including in complexity and in multiple locations, the pressure in that direction builds up.

A new leader often has the opportunity to question and redefine a unit's strategy. If such an opportunity exists, you should take it. Wise strategies emerge from careful analysis of what has, and has not, worked well to date, from listening to colleagues' aspirations and to the hopes of senior central officers and external friends.

Consider what is expected. A strategy? A business plan? A planning statement? A list of objectives? Over what time scales? How radical can you be? Is it best to question all assumptions even if it becomes clear that some actions are not realistic options. For example, it might be consistent with the strengths and aspirations of most of the staff to abandon undergraduate teaching so as to concentrate on postgraduate and post-experience teaching. Why not suggest that the institution should consult the funding council to trade some funded places? Maybe the HEI itself would find this too radical a step and one which would be inconsistent with the plans of the rest of the institution. Maybe the move would also be against the wishes of a considerable minority of the unit's own staff. Just considering the question will have been worthwhile since it is about assessing distinctive competence. In an overcrowded higher education sector, for how long will it make sense for most HEIs to operate in most subjects at most levels?

In academia, radical plans are often not appreciated, and for good reasons. Not only is there a more conservative mind-set and an effective operating horizon of several years (for example between one round of the RAE and the next, or from devising a new degree scheme through publicizing it, filling places and then seeing the first intake graduate), but also it is normally too risky or otherwise too difficult to staff up to run new ventures. Therefore, existing staff have to be transferred away from existing work which is a source of income. Hence all the metaphors about the difficulty of slowing or turning the ocean liner apply fully to higher education. To be fast on one's feet may mean that a field of activity has to be located in an entrepreneurial division in which staff have flexible contracts, renewal of which is contingent upon business success. This does not mean that the bulk of the enterprise can continue to grind on without change. The changes may be radical ones but it is essential that they are carefully planned in order to ensure that core work is maintained and that income streams are protected while action to ensure long-term security unfolds. The kind of incremental change which is required in many, if not most, sectors of higher education make a compelling case for the use of a strategic plan. The inherent forces for inertia, if combined with 'drift' or the lack of a plan, can cripple an organization and render it incapable of responding, even slowly, other than in crisis mode when severe damage may already have occurred.

Some academics have become adept at answering the questions when they receive an annual request to update their unit's strategy. This can turn into an academic exercise in the worst sense, not really engaging creative thought or commitment, and serving as a substitute for a strategy. Good reasons are produced to defend this process of opting out: success in the commercial world sometimes appears to result from opportunism or happenstance rather than from the working through of a carefully constructed plan; defining a strategic plan with numbers, dates and targets is viewed as a hostage to fortune. Credibility might be undermined if the unit fails to meet its targets, possibly weakening its political position within the institution. Specifying targets which are then approved also tends to locate responsibility with individuals to act and act effectively. This is an uncomfortable situation for some people and they strive to avoid it.

None of the above reasons for avoiding wrestling with a strategy carry much weight. If successes occur in the absence of a strategy, then no one will be sure whether they occurred by skill, effort or chance, and how they might be understood, replicated or extended. Were they due to one or more individuals, or to concerted actions on a broader front, or to national or international circumstances? If setbacks occur, their nature, timing and causes may not be understood if outcomes cannot be related to a plan.

A strategy need not contain multiple goals and targets to two decimal places. When many variables are outside the control of the unit, details can be specious, particularly when viewing the far end of a long planning horizon. In those circumstances, there is a danger that numbers are inserted merely to feed a central planner's spreadsheet. However, the strategy should contain sufficient substance to inform all members of the unit, especially those who are newly appointed or outside the main forum of decision making, of the context in which he or she is working. Everyone should know:

- in which directions the unit is applying its resources
- in which directions changes are likely to occur
- why such changes are occurring.

Why is it important for these points to be widely known? First, so that members of staff can see and understand how their individual efforts fit in with the work of the unit as a whole. Second, they – and indeed everyone up to the most senior levels in the unit – should receive guidance about the choices which are presented. Should we bid for that consultancy contract, or a research council grant? Should we let our postgraduate diploma programme die a natural death? If so, should we redevelop it as a Masters programme, redevelop some of the material as undergraduate options, or abandon the whole subject and move into an area of higher demand? Should we accept this slightly dubious applicant for a PhD? Should I agree to take on a quarter-time pastoral role in a hall of residence in exchange for my department's receiving a specified payment? Should I agree to organize an international conference here next year? These and many other choices are constantly presented to members of the unit. The staff can assess their own comparative strengths but to make rational choices, they need at least general indications of where the interests of their unit lie and how best to maximize the benefits to the unit and to their own career.

In proposing, or in requesting others to propose, strategies it is important not to waste people's time by asking for exact data which are not available, even approximately. Sensitivity of plans to events should be considered as part of a set of contingencies. This idea might not come naturally to academics who tend to prefer a single, elegant model. The unit will be so much the stronger if it has a sense of a portfolio of activities, so that some may be expanded if problems arise in other areas. Neither should a unit be criticized if it advocates varying strategies such as efficient, high volume and undifferentiated teaching in one sphere, alongside small-scale expensive provision in another – provided that its market analysis seems sound and well adapted to its capacity to deliver.

Central planners have to make the difficult judgement of whether it matters if one unit has a strategy markedly different from other units. Will the institution's whole profile, reputation, not to mention its marketing strategy, be undermined if it is seen to be pursuing different objectives in different subject groups? A desire to preserve consistency will of course limit choices for the units which are set up to run along essentially predetermined lines. However, since the expansion of the sector, institutions are more likely to encompass non-traditional activities or to work on multiple sites – circumstances which place pressure in the direction of more variety and more locally determined decision making. Also most markets are as specialized as ever, making it irrelevant for a sponsor or a student in subject X to know or care about standards at that institution in subject Y. For these reasons, central agencies such as the funding councils and the Quality Assurance Agency (QAA) for Higher Education have become increasingly insistent that institutions should have sound methods of corporate planning and of quality assurance to hold together what may be an increasingly diverse portfolio.

It is important that the strategic plan should not become an end in itself. If it turns into an 'exercise', then there will be a sense that once approved it is 'all done' until next year's revisions. It will be shelved, then dusted off, rather than being referred to and occasionally challenged whenever an issue arises. It should be a 'living' document as close as possible to the real concerns of the unit. If it progresses as a draft through all the committee and discussion phases with little debate or disagreement, then it is likely that a dead document has been created: a relevant strategy will attract plenty of comment and interest groups will compete for coverage and recognition within it.

The dean will be seen as responsible for the strategy and will be called upon to defend it. Certainly it should not be written by committee since that would cause messages to lose clarity amid a set of compromises. The document should be written by the dean and may first be drafted by a senior administrator. The process leading to the writing should entail the leaders of the unit listening to each other and to their colleagues and in gathering data from outside the institution. Before the leaders roll out the strategy and begin to implement it, they should be sure that they can count upon the support of most of their colleagues and that they and others can be inspired by the prospects and targets they have specified. There is no point in laying out objectives which are beyond both sight and grasp: a sense of failure is virtually inevitable. There is even less point in signing up for minimalist objectives. This would presumably be done for the sake of a quiet, undemanding life, but it would do nothing to engender commitment and a sense of achievement. Objectives which are within sight but just outside one's grasp are often thought to be most appropriate to a strategy.

Another important piece of advice, obvious to some, is to 'start from where you're at'. Look around at the resources you already have at your disposal and consider the extent to which they can be improved during the life of the strategic plan. You have to make best use of all your resources, including some which you might prefer to replace but which will remain with you in the medium to long term. For example, you will achieve nothing by declaring academic research to be your unit's leading objective if you are basing it on the 15 per cent of your staff who are currently research active. Unless the age structure indicates that a massive clear-out is about to occur through retirements, you will only chip away at your 85 per cent non-researchers. The strategy might sound good, but it will alienate the majority who are unable and unwilling to contribute to the research strategy and you are unlikely to be able to show much progress when the strategy is reviewed.

For most academic units, radical change is possible only within a defined unit, such as a research centre or a group delivering post-experience teaching and consultancy, or over a long period. The dean may have to plan for improvements which will stretch well beyond his or her tenure, in which case sharing the strategy with colleagues and prospective successors is essential. Embedding the strategy is a requirement without which even an active, successful period of deanship may be seen in the long term as a brief illuminated interlude amid a pattern of mediocrity.

Collaboration ■

An important consideration in drafting a strategy is the extent to which the unit may wish to collaborate, either with other units at the institution or with others elsewhere. Joint teaching programmes have obvious potential to extend the range of provision and so tap into new sources of demand. Joint research has potential to push back conventional subject barriers. Yet it is normally the case that units find one another somewhat difficult to work with and that collaborative research tends to be uphill work. Modular degree schemes enable some joint programmes to be offered without the pains, or benefits, of truly collaborative provision. Events of recent years have made internal collaboration more difficult: the RAE has tended to channel research into established disciplines, teaching quality assessment and quality control processes have demanded a lot of attention within a unit – which is likely to be multidisciplinary in itself – thus reducing the collective appetite for initiating joint programmes with other units. The 'audit culture' is also in danger of discouraging enterprising academics from engaging in innovative inter-institutional collaboration.

However, the possibilities of joint ventures with a counterpart unit at another institution may nevertheless be attractive. If the collaborative partner is based in the locality, then savings might be achieved through joint teaching of small courses, rationalizing provision to eliminate duplication of effort, sharing library or IT facilities, or maximizing the use of classrooms. Such measures might succeed if the two institutions are in harmony: if they are unalike, then only some of the economies will be attainable. If they are alike and in the same locality, then the collaboration may prefigure a more substantial relationship, or even a merger.

More distant collaboration based on *complementary strengths* may be more appropriate for some. The distinctive strength of one institution may enable it to act as a feeder to the other institution which thereby reaches a market it would not otherwise easily penetrate. One might provide to the other a regional base at low cost. Such arrangements are most likely to be attractive if the institutions are not in direct competition with each other and if they enjoy a parity of esteem in their various markets. Such relationships, particularly if they involve validation and are conducted overseas, may absorb an unduly large amount of academic and administrative time in quality control procedures. However, if the benefits are substantial (and they might include intangibles such as a reputation enhanced by association with a well-respected partner institution), then a joint venture can provide a valuable extension of the portfolio.

Strategy for change

Each academic unit has both to work out its own preferences for development and to relate them to the rest of the institution. Tensions are likely to arise, unless the HEI operates as a 'holding company' for a set of units which essentially determine their own destiny and achieve agreed objectives in their own way. Such a model might best apply to a relatively large, successful institution in which high standards are likely to be achieved across the board. If there are areas of significant underperformance, then a different approach is necessary. This may entail the institution's placing a particular unit on a recovery track, closely monitoring its performance and insisting on supervising both its policies and its methods of achieving its objectives. If its underperformance has a financial aspect, then the rest of the institution will in effect be cross-subsidizing it and so will naturally have an interest in seeing its problems solved.

Between the above relatively extreme positions are more likely eventualities. Each unit is likely to be battling for an improved share of resources or, indeed, seeking more resources so that it can generate additional income. In such bargaining situations, the unit which has a set of intentions, a strategy or a business plan will tend to hold an advantage over other units, particularly if their lack of such plans is the result of wishing to maintain their share with minimum disturbance and a marked reluctance to change or engage in new forms of activity. Central bodies may push units to engage in new work, for example collaborative teaching or research with another internal unit. Some such ideas may not make best sense to the units themselves but they may have to accommodate them in order to deal with the political reality. Units with no convincing plans are more vulnerable to being 'pushed' in this fashion.

In difficult financial circumstances, the conservative tendencies of most academic leaders tend to predominate. Efforts are made to preserve time for research and priority is given to teaching established, familiar programmes, even if the signs are that the market is declining and that new forms of provision should be identified. Staff have become accustomed to erosion in the unit of resource so further cuts tend not to produce a sense of urgency – more a resigned determination to stick to the knitting in the knowledge that previous years' cuts were not actually disastrous. What is going on is a kind of voluntary euthanasia, a slow death. In the medium term, quality will fall markedly, even if no dramatic closures or financial crashes occur. In order to arrest the decline, decisive action is required, either from the centre of the institution, which may impose a solution upon the unit, or from within. In such circumstances, deans have to be champions of change. It is no longer sufficient to keep knocking 5 per cent off the stationery budget. Some escape from the downward spiral is required, and this normally means increasing income rather than further reductions in expenditure. It also tends to entail risk, perhaps setting up new operations at considerable expense with no guarantee of pay-back and the probability of deficits in the short term. Therefore, courage and persuasiveness are also needed. In order to succeed, the academic unit will have to identify 'project champions' who are released from the normal constraints of progressing their career through research and teaching and given other incentives to make things happen. Once new activities are focused around one individual or a small team, they gain at least provisional credibility. Without a group of champions, properly commissioned, coordinated, led and rewarded, any strategy for change – however elegant or precise it may appear on paper – is doomed to fail.

It is tempting to believe that the ability to produce a convincing strategic or business plan is crucially important. It is not. While advice can be given about what should or should not be included within such plans, paperwork is no substitute for reality. The leaders of the unit have first to assess their situation and listen carefully to their colleagues at all levels to determine what will and what will not motivate them. There will be an exception to this only if a major turnover of staff is about to happen and there is an opportunity for significant new recruitment.

At the same time, the leaders must understand the environment, both in the outside world and within the institution, so that the unit may try to align itself with others' expectations and decide which opportunities it should pursue. And which it should ignore. The notion of priorities is fundamental to strategy. In higher education, the natural tendency of many staff is to be inclusive, accepting subjects, ideas and projects as valid and valuable. A new centre springs up because some seed-corn funding is available, an established programme continues even though it has ceased to be financially viable, links with HEIs in the Third World are created even though they cost time and money because someone believes that there may be long-term benefits. In some cases, people are willing to support ventures because they are a 'good thing' which the institution 'ought' to do. Rational arguments are scarcely applicable once this mind-set becomes established.

The amount of staff resource available is fixed, or at least finite. In order to make the most of new opportunities, staff time must be released. Almost certainly, unless the unit has been generously staffed, some other activities must be 'managed downwards', by gaining greater efficiencies in their running, scaling them down or by with-drawing from them altogether. The sensitivities associated with reordering priorities should not be underestimated, particularly in a case where a group of staff are redeployed from an activity they value highly towards other work which the unit, but not those staff, sees as more important. The leaders then face a challenge – not necessarily insurmountable – to remotivate some or all of that group.

Time-scale is essential to a strategy. It is tempting, in response to others' eager expectations, to commit oneself to deadlines which may later prove unattainable. An unnecessary sense of failure is the result if it takes longer than planned to create new operations and make them run successfully. Change in higher education is usually incremental. This is particularly the case where the desired change is to a mainstream activity. It is possible to carry out a quick fix on a teaching programme, giving it a new title and rearranging the modules and methods of assessment. If the reality has not changed, then any benefits may be gained only in the short term. If it is really not a very good programme, it will not attract many good students. Evidence, such as from the Weatherhead School of Management at Case Western Reserve University in Cleveland, Ohio, is that genuine curricular change can take something like seven years. Its lead product, the Master of Business Administration (MBA), was reviewed from bottom to top and all the teaching staff had to be brought on board, convinced of the need for change, then engaged in hard background work to recreate the programme. A strategic plan will be the more convincing to outsiders, and acceptable to one's own staff, if it is shown to be moving steadily at a pace where the direction can be adjusted in response to circumstances. A headlong rush often ends at the bottom of a cliff. Naturally, it can be difficult to sustain momentum when change is long term and it is a key function for leaders of the unit to keep reminding colleagues that they are engaged on a journey to a particular destination. The metaphor is imperfect because, by the nature of institutions, the destination constantly moves ahead and the journey becomes perpetual. More important for staff is the sense of continuous improvement and the reward which comes with successful outcomes. When disappointments occur, they can be placed into the context of a larger enterprise and so be less damaging to morale.

When making difficult journeys, it is advisable to be aware of escape routes and less challenging alternatives. Any strategy should contain contingency plans even if they assume that one has to think the unthinkable. It may be an uncomfortable thought that your research rating could fall from 5 to 3 or that recruitment to your main teaching programme may be halved. And what if *both* events occur? How could you respond if 85 per cent of your staffing commitments are to people on permanent contracts? Some reactions might be of use in the short term only, for example by buying no new computers and library books or by cutting out travel to conferences. Others might form part of a change of strategic direction; perhaps certain staff could switch into carrying out more contract research and consultancy or early retirement packages might be offered to selected higher paid staff. Other costs might be attacked, for instance sell your building and relocate to smaller or shared premises. In times of crisis, external solutions can be overlooked. Are other units in similar circumstances and what might be achieved by pooling resources?

Analysing contingencies may often include considering how to avoid dependence on specific sources of income. Ideally 80 per cent of your international students should not originate from the same country, 80 per cent of your corporate income should not be derived from one company and 80 per cent of your research income should not come from a single sponsor. Your organization is volatile and subject to change. Others are more so. A change of director, an adverse set of accounts or a government directive may be enough to remove your income stream in shorter order than you can cope with. You could then face the negative end of a Pareto effect: you have lost 80 per cent of your income and are left with having to exert 80 per cent of your effort to earn the 20 per cent which remains.

Should such dependence be avoided? After all, large contracts are evidence of success, of having persuaded another organization of your quality and ability to deliver, and they probably allow you to reap economies of scale by using your knowledge of that organization to operate effectively by repeat or large-volume work. Those contracts also make strategic sense if they correspond to your mission and to the core skills of your staff. They are evidence of keeping focused on areas of strength.

Clearly your organization must have sufficient staffing (critical mass) both to service the core work effectively and to extend into other activities. Even long-term projects have a short life by institutional standards, and the pace of change is increasing. Although larger units are more vulnerable because of their higher level of fixed or semi-fixed costs, they have the advantage of being able to diversify their risks through a balanced portfolio of work. Ideally, at least some of the staff will be capable of switching between activities. Secretaries are normally fully flexible, most administrators are flexible, academic staff less so. If lecturers can readily adapt their material between various audiences (first-year undergraduates, final-year undergraduates, postgraduates on generalist programmes, postgraduates on specialist programmes, graduate trainees in companies, leading senior managers in companies) you have a great advantage. In this case, only an exceptional lecturer will be able to span the full range and do so successfully.

The natural tendency in academic units is towards specialization at the individual level and a permissive culture which values virtually all activities. Hence to push for a broad portfolio is usually to push at an open door so far as academic staff are concerned. The success of the strategy may also be size dependent and resource dependent. Thus one may be able to run a new MBA programme only if a specialist department can grow from six to nine and so represent a satisfactory range of expertise.

Ideally, within the portfolio might be activities which prosper in different circumstances. For example, some teaching programmes (such as the MBA) tend to flourish when the economy is expanding and prospects for promotion in business are improving. Others (for example some specialist Masters programmes) run counter to the economic cycle and tend to attract most applications when graduate employment prospects are poor and students see the advantages of adding vocationally relevant skills to their first degree and of delaying their entry into the job market. Both types of programmes are unlikely to peak together or slump together. The leaders of the unit have the task of balancing narrowness and overdependence (a short-term harvest which risks future famine) against dissipation of effort and loss of focus on priorities. The continuous task of forming a strategy requires periodic statements which summarize it at specific moments. Here is an example of a framework for such a summary.

Box 4.1 Case study of a strategy of a leading business school in the US

Mission

To enhance the practice of management through education and research

Goal

To BE and to be RECOGNIZED as one of the ten best graduate business schools

The competition

(14 other schools listed)

Recognized by primary constituencies

Business community
Academic community
Student applicants
The media

For

Programmes: MBA, PhD, executive education
Research: basic, applied

	Business community	Academic community	Applicants	Media
Importance to us	detail	detail	detail	detail
Expectations of us	detail	detail	detail	detail
Measures of our accomplishment	detail	detail	detail	detail
Strategies to achieve our goals	detail	detail	detail	detail

Hurdles in the environment

(list)

Strengths of the school

(list)

Challenges

People: the key to quality
Endowment: the capital to ensure quality

Strategies	People	Endowment
	Detail on hiring of faculty, recruitment of students and working with business leaders	Detail on raising endowment income

5

STAFF ROLES

What are the key roles? Where are the pressure points within the unit and at the interface with the centre of the institution?

The dean/director

The dean or director is normally the leader of the unit and its representative on key institutional decision-making bodies. Large, externally oriented units such as business schools have been known to split the internal and external leadership roles by appointing a dean for internal business as well as a director to represent the unit externally. This can be an effective method of making an overwhelming workload manageable, but it is essential that the two post-holders act hand-in-glove, otherwise major problems can arise.

The role of dean is potentially stressful because of conflicting pressures – both from colleagues whose interests are to be represented to the powers that be, and from the centre of the institution, since the dean will normally be a member of the senior management team which takes 'cabinet responsibility' and a whole-institution perspective. Deciding how strongly to press the claims of their own departments and conveying unwelcome messages from the centre to the troops are likely to be everyday experiences for deans.

In times of crisis, the balance can shift decisively towards central direction. For example, the unit may find that its claims for replacement appointments are delayed or vetoed, despite the protests of the dean, who may in turn be tasked with implementing cost savings in the unit. At such times the dean may appear to the constituents to be an ineffectual negotiator or an agent of central control.

It is not surprising that deans have been known to lose the support of heads of department, and eventually the role itself, through
being perceived to be ineffective in delivering resources or through
being the bringer of bad news once too often.

The problem of finding people willing to act as heads of department (see below) is writ large in the case of the top job. In US
business schools – admittedly one of the most pressurized fields –
there was an annual turnover of 24 per cent in the dean position in
the late 1980s (Wholihan 1990; *Fortune* 1994). The situation has
almost certainly become even more fraught: in April 1998, there
were 71 deans' jobs waiting to be filled in North American business
schools alone (*Financial Times*, 20 April 1998). It seems that the
institutions which experience the greatest change are often among
the most prestigious for it is in those places where stakeholders are
the most demanding.

Continuity and progress are hampered in all fields by a lack of
senior people willing to take on dean and director positions. In the
UK, the root cause is almost certainly the continuing reluctance within
the system to recognize academic leadership as a serious career choice.

The dean, in any subject, is increasingly cast in the role of agent
of change – whether in relation to the curriculum or internal processes. Since academics normally resist change, a dean who intends
to achieve things will almost inevitably experience opposition,
whether temporary or otherwise.

The scenario is not always so bleak. In good times, the dean may
bring in new business in the form of sponsorship, research grants or
contracts, or full-cost teaching programmes. Success in one area of
the institution can raise morale for the rest and trigger affordable
expansion in staffing or building.

The dean may be appointed by the head of the institution, following varying degrees of consultation with the staff in the unit. The
appointment might follow an external advertisement. Alternatively,
the dean might be elected, either by the heads of departments comprising the unit or by all members of the unit. The nature of the
appointment is likely to make a major difference to everyone's
expectations. For example, if appointed rather than elected, the dean
may be in post for an indefinite period; if elected, the dean is more
likely to serve for a fixed period of three to five years. In a permanent position, the dean is likely to feel that he or she is expected by
all concerned to make a distinctive mark and to have a relatively
free hand to make changes. With a nearer horizon, the dean may
be constrained by concerns about today's commitments becoming
tomorrow's headaches for the next dean, or by a desire not to make
enemies prior to returning to a regular position on the faculty.

It would be absurd to suggest that one's success as a dean is conditioned by one's job description. Sometimes institutional ambiguity can facilitate success. For example, some HEIs have a faculty structure grafted on to a department-based system. Formal power is not taken away from the heads of department, who remain directly answerable to the vice-chancellor and the Senate, but a dean of faculty is interposed with the clear expectation that the dean will act on behalf of the faculty as a collective unit. In a host of everyday matters, the dean has to give a faculty view and to exercise judgements which are not equally acceptable to all the constituent departments. The heads of department may in effect and implicitly agree to surrender their power of veto in the confidence that their long-term interests lie with the direction being followed by the larger unit of which they form a part. However, if the dean should lose the confidence of the heads of department, they might call upon their powers of veto and find ways to destabilize the dean who might, or might not, then receive the backing of the vice-chancellor and pro-vice-chancellors.

This kind of ambiguous model cannot be recommended because it relies too heavily upon the personal qualities of the individuals involved. An institution which is convinced of the merits of a management system which devolves significant decisions to faculty level should ensure that the deans have the formal and explicit support from the top and that it is made clear to the members of the unit concerned that they have to make their case to their dean.

What are the alternatives to devolution to faculty level? The first is to impose central control over virtually all decisions, making the dean – if appointed – little more than an administrative conduit. The problem with this model is that it stifles creativity at the grass roots and creates a potentially confrontational them-versus-us relationship between academic staff and the central administration, which tends to be an expensive operation because it requires a large staff to implement its all-embracing procedures.

A second model is to devolve, but to devolve to a level lower than that of the faculty – perhaps to departments or even to research or teaching groups. As the system has expanded and external demands upon it have grown, few if any institutions believe that it is feasible to permit the inevitable fragmentation and duplication which this entails. Allocating resources to 5 or 6 major units is a very different process from allocating resources to 50 or 60 departments, some of which are too small to manage the organization of their own affairs.

The sector has been influenced since the late 1970s by practice in the outside world, which has been to reduce the power of bureaucracies in favour of their subsidiary business units. Real power – and real accountability – have been located at lower levels, not only to encourage a more responsive attitude towards customers but also to reduce the cost of decisions moving up and down chains of command. HEIs have looked at the size and diversity of their operations and all but the smallest and most narrowly focused have concluded that, in order to be cost-effective, they require decisions to be taken by soundly based relatively large units, working within agreed institutional guidelines and processes. The choices they have made, influenced by history and culture, have led to variability in the degree of effective devolution and in a range of activities from staff appointments through budget control to facilities management, but few people disagree that substantial delegation of responsibility to the level of the faculty or large school is the most appropriate model for the present and foreseen future. The following two examples give a brief insight into the daunting challenges of deanship. The first is from one of the leading business schools in the US, the second is from a British post-1992 university.

When I think about curricular reform and improvement at Michigan, what I mainly feel is tremendous pride in a number of people who were willing to take risks, to step out and try new and different things. Some were in the dean's office, but most were department chairs and individuals on the faculty.

What were the important lessons you learned from this experimentation?
I'll give you a very specific one, and that's the importance of the word 'pilot'. We found that if we presented big programmatic change to the faculty – big change along the lines of 'Here is the old world, and here is the new world. We want you in the new world, and you can never go back' – everybody froze up. But if we approached change piece by piece – by introducing, for example, seven-week instead of fourteen-week courses, the MAP [Management Assistance Project] program, executive skills, training for a new orientation – almost nobody could reasonably disagree without giving it a try. So virtually everything we did was on a pilot basis. We said to the faculty, 'Let's do this for a couple of years. Let's agree now that there will be a review, and if we don't like it we'll either go back to what we had or modify it further.' This seemed to free people up, and of course the truth is that when you change you never completely go back.

There's been a lot of modification, fine-tuning of the pretty rough concepts we put in place initially.

A second important lesson we learned is the vital importance of leadership. These things wouldn't have gotten done without individual people from the dean's office, faculty, and staff who accepted full responsibility. We came to realize that while we needed the support of our regular faculty, we couldn't get all of it done with regular faculty alone. Supplemental faculty and staff have taken on an amazingly important role in the change process here, because our education and development model requires tasks that regular faculty can't or don't want to do. An example is creation of all those partnerships with companies in the MAP program to provide sixty high-quality fieldwork experiences. There are several senior staff people who have been invaluable, both in understanding the academic concept of what we've been doing and in getting out there in the real world and lining up the companies.

What management style works best for you at Michigan?
I think the involved party may be the least capable of answering that question, but I'll try to give you an answer. There are three or four principles that guide me. Number one, I believe deeply in the power of high aspirations. I once heard Bob Galvin reflect on Motorola's change and improvement, saying that the single most important thing he did was to always challenge the organization to be the best it could be.

The second guiding principle is to select excellent people to be the leaders of the school. When I compare universities and business schools to the experience I had in corporate life, the single most serious and widespread mistake I see is deans settling for people on their staffs who are less than excellent. When you decide whom you're going to rely on to make things happen, you've set a ceiling on how good it's going to be. I have been really fortunate to be able to recruit some absolutely superb people to take on leadership roles in the school as associate deans, area chairs, and heads of critical committees.

My third principle is what I call 'the presumption of yes.' In business schools today we're surrounded by talented people with all kinds of ideas. If you're a dean, you have to be able to find ways to say yes instead of no to the many ideas that come your way. We all know that fresh ideas are very fragile. If they don't get reinforcement, they dry up very quickly. And it's not just financial reinforcement; it's interest and appreciation and recognition. I've often told our students that this is not like a Broadway play, with the students as the audience and the faculty and administration on the stage. We're all in it together, and the school's going to be as good as we make it together.

We've received an amazing outpouring of good ideas from our students. We cannot implement all of them, but when we can't we always explain why.

(Graduate Management
Admission Council 1998: 24–5)

Being a Dean in a new university is not like being a Dean in an old one. You aren't, for instance, voted in by colleagues for a three-year stint, afterwards to fall back with relief into the library to resume your research. It's a full-time, permanent management post, usually 'third-tier', senior to everyone except the Vice-Chancellors and their Deputies. Deans run Faculties. They may also carry cross-institutional responsibilities: mine are to be a member of the University's Executive (Vice-Chancellor and Deputies, Deans and Divisional Heads) and to chair its Teaching and Learning Policy Committee.

Most of our professors are researchers whose work justifies the label which proclaims that they profess their discipline at its highest level. Many Deans also carry the title 'Professor' and some may do so by virtue of their research. Others, myself included, carry it more as an honorific, the post I applied for not having been advertised as a research post. The justification, I suppose, is that anyone who achieves what it takes to become a Dean is, by definition, 'distinguished' enough to warrant the title. I like the versatility of the 'new' universities in their preparedness to admit other people as professors than only those who are eminent researchers. However, I fear that, as the differences between 'new' and 'old' begin to blur, research is becoming the only criterion which really seems to count. Though our professors mix the various ingredients of distinction (teaching, management, track-record, etc) in different measures, most overwhelm the other flavours with the piquancy of their research. What's more, though some may pull it off, I don't believe it's possible for many of us to be both Deans and significant researchers at the same time. The work-load is heavy; though moving through seasonal changes, it is unremitting; and its nature means that one must be prepared for constant interruptions, unexpected deadlines, sudden crises. I long ago learned that the occasional 'empty' day in the diary was the most dangerously deceptive of all, for it is invariably the one in which such crises occur. Were I to spend, say, half my time pensive and curious in the Library, my Faculty would cease to function. (At least I hope it would.)

The day-job, then, is running the Faculty. Some numbers here may be helpful, to get a sense of the scale of the thing. My Faculty (Arts and Education) operates on two of the University's four campuses, together with two city-centre annexes, ten miles apart from each other and sixty miles from head office. We teach some 2,500 full-time undergraduates in three modular degree programmes, together with about a hundred students on our PGCE [Postgraduate Certificate in Education]. At postgraduate, post-experience level, we have close to 1,300 students on modular part-time routes which can lead to Masters. We have approaching 50 MPhil/PhD students. We have distant oversight of about another thousand students working at diploma or undergraduate level on franchised programmes in other institutions. A hundred or so students a year study with us from countries abroad. We employ about 120 academic staff, together with part-time staff (everyone from visiting professors to life-models) counted not as separate genetic entities but as 'part time hours', so I don't know how many there are. We have around 35 administrative staff and 25 technicians. It is a large undertaking costing many millions a year, money for which I am responsible (and ultimately sackable if I get it wrong).

I run the Faculty with a senior team consisting of four Heads of School (who also take whole-Faculty responsibilities), and Heads of Research and Faculty Administration. I also bring three members of the non-promoted lecturing staff on to the Faculty Executive on a two- or three-year rotation in order to ensure that there's a 'grass roots' influence in our decision-making. All the academic decisions are taken in committees and boards with elected representatives working alongside the *ex-officio* members (those who have to be there by virtue of their position within the Faculty).

That's the width: what of the quality? One way to describe what I actually do is to say that I *preside over* (the verb is probably not a perfect expression of reality) the process of recruitment, induction, teaching, assessment and graduation of all our students; over the appointment, appraisal, development and sometimes promotion of all our staff; over the management and distribution of all our money and our other resources; and over the allocation and safety management of all our teaching space (though I don't carry responsibility for the estates themselves, nor for their upkeep and maintenance, nor for the central services – like Library, catering, residence, etc – which attend the functions of each Faculty). I preside over the formulation, management and outcome of our research; over the curriculum; over the syllabuses; over the way we organize ourselves into groupings of various kinds to do various jobs; over the quality assurance processes; over our relationships with the rest of the University, and with the other educational agencies with which we work. I preside over the many rhetorics and arguments, disagreements and alliances which make up a large and complex sub-organization within the University. I am supposed to offer the words which will best express to others our many purposes, and in this sense I preside over the Faculty's 'philosophy'. I preside over its people, inasmuch as a great deal of my time is spent in knowing about and trying to assist staff. I preside over its morale.

'Preside over' because, of course, I don't do all these things myself, but I have to ensure that someone else does, and must also be satisfied that they do them well. In fact, I try to encourage other people to do as many of them as possible. But Deans here are supposed to be in charge of all this, and if things go wrong then ultimately it's they who must accept responsibility.

Deans also initiate. I'm never quite convinced that one of the laws of clever management is to make people think it was their idea all along (though sometimes that works well, and often it also happens to be true). If Deans never had any ideas of their own, I suspect people would quickly wonder what they drew their salaries for. But having ideas is only the start of the process: it's much harder to get people to support them, and then move them into a realized, practical reality. Time can sometimes be important here: when my faculty was first formed (as the result, four years ago, of two faculties merging) I spent the first three months consulting widely among its members on how we should organize ourselves, deciding upon a School structure. One of the Schools (consisting of a wide range of disparate subjects) was difficult to name, and eventually I chose *Humanities and Cultural Interpretation*. 'After all,' said one member of staff, 'interpreting culture is what we all do, isn't it?' I always hoped that the 'cultural interpretation' idea would move further than just to exist as the second half of a title, at the time believing that the processes of interpreting our own and other cultures was complex, compelling, difficult and worthy of study. Four years on, groups of people in that School, working with others in the Faculty, are beginning to plan a new degree pathway, probably to be called *Cultural Interpretation and Practice*. This – if it comes off – is a good example of initiating unobtrusively – and patiently.

Deans also react. Having teacher education as a significant part of my Faculty means that we react on a twice-weekly basis, these days, to the latest consultation document from the Teacher Training Agency or Ofsted. We often ask why we bother, for the good it does, but like the party you don't want to go to, but feel you have to be seen at, so with these documents: we feel we should respond for fear that, one day, their worst excesses may come to haunt us if we don't. Certainly, teacher education is currently the most embattled part of higher education, as government quangos do their best to suffocate it with perverse bureaucracy. Our response strategy reminds me of those gardeners working at the turn of the century on the Great Estate who ensured that their asparagus beds were *perfectly* aligned, at an angle of *exactly* 45° as a way of showing their contempt for the man for whom they worked and the aristocratic system he represented. Find the fault in *that*, you bastards, but don't think it makes the slightest difference to the taste of the asparagus!

Higher education is a process, marked along the way by a series of products. Deans profess to understand how this process works, and how they can coerce it to the benefit of those they manage and represent. The products are what testify to their ability, or otherwise, to influence the process. There are a great many products: numbers of students recruited successfully to target; quality of their degree outcomes; amount of money earned from sources other than the funding council (research grants, Quality Research (QR) money, etc); staff who gain promotion, within or outside the institution; PhD completions; good examiners' reports . . . these are regulars. Also countable are the absence of things: a low complaints count from people in the neighbourhood about students' street behaviour is one; from those within the Faculty about anything at all another; low drop-out rates a third. We live in a world where worth is counted in measures like these, and Deans are held responsible.

Yet the real values are more definable in terms of the processes over which Deans preside. Do people feel they have somewhere to go with good ideas? Is morale high or low? Are our academic freedoms defended when attacked? Are our standards high? What do visitors to the Faculty say about us: are there impressionistic measures we can use to see how well, or badly, we are working? What's life like outside the lecture room: are special events well-attended, like evening research seminars and occasional conferences? A Faculty is like a piece of hardware: it's an organizational device which aims to amplify all the virtues which higher education can offer for a sub-set of the University's community. The software is more complex: the people who work and study in it, and the ideas and knowledge, the skills and understanding they acquire and practise and test against accountable standards. Each summer, people leave the machine for other places, and the machine remains behind, albeit changed (subtly or significantly) by their process through it. Deans are the ones responsible for the nature of the machine, and for the quality of much of its software.

I sometimes look back to my time as an undergraduate (York, 1964–67). The people who ran 'new' universities in those days had a different task. It seems that Government said unto them: 'Here's a green-field site close to a great and ancient city of much beauty, and here is some money. Go and build a university.' (The famous story at the time was that the iconic water-tower at the University of York had been designed on the back of a beer mat by the vice-chancellor, Lord James of Rusholme, during a good night out, and lo! it came to be erected much as the sketch indicated.) That kind of higher education has gone, and some of the management skills needed to make it successful are less prominent now, while other, newer, ones have come to dominate. I wonder how Lord James and his colleagues would have managed things in the 1990s, the very point in my own career development where I happen to have reached a relatively senior position in this university. I like to think (I could be wrong) that they'd have foundered, that the constant battle against eroding resources and the need to be forever accountable would have seen them off in their first term. Indeed, knowing then what we know today, I suspect that many of these energetic and inspiring people, burning with the excitement of their vision for university education in the 1960s, would never have allowed themselves to come within a mile of university management today. Too depressing!

But then again, the vision is not so different now, just different in scale. We're here to help people develop themselves as far as they can go, to become members of a community marked by knowledge and intellectual curiosity and confidence of action, leading for a few into the world of research, and for most into a useful, purposeful life in a complex modern democracy. We're giving our students a fuller and more precise set for tools for their lives. Just as universities did in the 1960s, but we're doing it for more people nowadays. Doing it in different ways. Doing it in a different society, and for a more extensive range of purposes. Being a Dean here, difficult though it is (maintenance more than building), is nonetheless a privilege. The people are

impressive, be they students or staff, and their purposes still
have dignity. In some ways, they have an added seriousness, too,
in comparison to that other higher education I look back to,
because their successes are achieved against higher odds. So I'll go
on professing that for a little while longer, assuming They let me.

(Newby 1997: 35–41)

Associate deans/directors

In larger units, it makes sense to create some division of labour
so that one person is not expected to shoulder the many varied
burdens of academic leadership. These might include generating
external income from commercial activities, fund-raising, networking with alumni, planning and leading a media relations campaign,
developing or redesigning teaching programmes, providing research
leadership, negotiating for resources from central bodies, proposing
and running budgets, implementing workload allocation models,
consulting with and being available to internal colleagues, benchmarking with other institutions including serving on external bodies, and
a host of ceremonial duties.

One or more associates, or a deputy, might take on some of the
roles described above, leaving the dean to concentrate on the matters which are deemed to hold highest priority or which correspond
to his or her strengths. It is customary, but by no means universal,
for associate deans to be drawn from the existing professorial staff
and to complete a 'tour of duty' of three years. A coherent set of
activities, such as staff and doctoral research, teaching programmes
and quality assurance, or staff workloads and other resources issues
are all areas which are sometimes delegated by the dean. Some
activities, including aspects of those listed above as falling within
an associate dean's portfolio, might be delegated to professional staff
(see Issues for administrators, pp. 63–6).

However, some post-1992 universities now advertise externally at
least some of their school-based associate dean roles. This seems
to be evidence of a growing administrative pathway for senior academic managers, a route to institutional leadership not necessarily
based upon eminence as a researcher. If it is the case that opportunities to develop leadership skills at associate dean level are increasing
and that 'associates' may thereby prepare for more substantial responsibility as deans, then an important building block is being put
into place. The lack of proper preparation for academic leadership
below the level of dean, or indeed at any level, is frequently remarked upon.

In order to ensure unity of purpose and agreed actions, the associate deans join the dean in a senior management team which meets frequently to act also as a steering group for the unit. In some schools, the team includes a senior administrator who is normally not formally a member, but whose job is to record, communicate and implement the team's decisions. It might also include other members, perhaps elected from the staff or in an *ex officio* capacity, but there is a risk with larger groups that effectiveness of decision making will be diluted. In any event, it is the dean and associate deans who form the core of the group.

Heads of department

Some schools are unidepartmental, so that the dean is in fact the head of department for the whole group. Other schools or faculties comprise several departments, each of which has its own head. In a large unit without constituent departments, it is highly likely that the dean will, or ought to, be supported by associate deans. If the constituent departments exist, then it is possible for the heads to form an extended management team with the dean and possibly also with associate deans.

An extended management team with heads of department is perhaps more a theoretical than a real possibility. In some faculties, the constituent departments are diverse and have little in common as disciplines: some have been assigned to a faculty as a matter of organizational convenience and do not fit. Even where the disciplines are closely aligned, the prospects for collaborative working may be even worse, particularly if there is a history of rivalry and turf warfare rather than joint endeavour.

Organization, as well as culture, can conspire against effectiveness at this level. Heads of department are normally elected by the members of the department or appointed by the head of the institution through the dean following consultation with the staff. Many have actively sought to avoid taking on the role, which they see as an unwelcome interruption to their research or teaching. Institutions cast the head in the role of line manager – a concept not accepted by many of the managed, nor by the managers! Without proper preparation or training, the head normally plays an important role in promotions issues, quality assurance, budget management, and the management of academic and non-academic staff, yet receives an allowance which is likely to be a pittance, an insultingly small compensation for the increased responsibilities which have to be handled. The head also has to fight the department's corner, if not in wider institutional circles, then within the faculty.

In a typical three-year stint, a new head spends the first year learning the system, the second year recovering from mistakes and redirecting matters, and the third year avoiding long-term changes and looking forward to returning to proper academic life.

Nor is the system satisfactory for the faculty or the institution as a whole. Although the head is supposed to represent the views of colleagues, which are not likely to change markedly within short periods of time, the reality is that some heads stamp their personality upon the role. One of the most disconcerting experiences for a dean or a faculty administrator is to find that the previous head of a department had set a standard of cooperation and efficiency which his or her successor has no intention of emulating.

It may well be that the traditional model has no long-term future. In smaller departments, chronic problems arise from sabbatical leave, the taking of which can prevent some courses being taught and some people from taking up headship duties. The impending prospect of being fingered for the headship is known to trigger dysfunctional behaviour, such as attempts at blackmail ('I'll only do it if I get . . .'). Once into the job, some heads are most unwilling to make waves internally because they will soon return to the body of the department and do not wish to damage their own long-term interests.

Some HEIs have analysed the difficulties associated with headship of departments, but solutions are difficult to find. The faculty model, in which departments are subordinate to a larger entity, has considerable advantages: the departments retain a distinctive academic and financial profile subject to also meeting faculty objectives; the HEI's costs are reduced by inserting a layer of management and dealing with it rather than with, say, seven or eight units in each faculty; in an effective faculty, opportunities for collaborative working with other departments are facilitated; and in a faculty which is collectively successful, each department is much less vulnerable than on a stand-alone basis.

Why retain departments at all? Wouldn't faculties be better off without the complication of multiple units which risk disharmony and duplication of effort? Before moving to a unidepartmental structure, bear in mind the loyalty factor. Especially in large schools and faculties, members of staff can relate much more easily to a group of colleagues (even if some of them are not like minded) from their own disciplinary background. They are less likely to feel loyalty to a larger unit, such as a faculty or, indeed, a college or university. Larger units – those with more than, say, 30 staff – tend in any case to form themselves unofficially into interest groups or cliques, so that even without a history of departments, academic groups tend to form them. There are other practical considerations. For example, imagine being the associate dean responsible for drawing up staff workloads for all 100 academic staff or for approving their financial transactions.

Research at the University of Uppsala on the role of heads of department suggests that the experience of doing the job is common across national boundaries. While collegial expectations tend to cast the head in the role of servant of the group, some staff nevertheless expect their head to show decisive leadership. This is one of the several potential conflicts which a head must manage. Others include disagreements between members of the department, competition for scarce resources and problems regarding individuals' performance.

The Uppsala researchers found that heads work an average of 50 hours a week and within each working day experience just over 80 per cent of all activities lasting 15 minutes or less. This picture of response to interruption and tolerance of fragmentary activity recalls the classic research carried out by Henry Mintzberg (1973) which showed that managers respond to frequent interruption, short-term activities, phone calls and hearsay, in preference to rational planning and written reports.

First experiences

It was my second or third day as Head of Department (HoD). The paper work quota for the day was finished. Time to put the feet up onto the desk and do some visionary thinking about where the subject was going and how we intended to stay at the forefront. The office door imploded and in stormed a cleaning lady, formidable beyond her early twenties. 'What are you going to do about the toilet roll holders in the men's toilets?' She saw the lack of an immediate response as a sign of weakness and proceeded to give me a fifteen minute harangue on the iniquities of life on the cleaning staff.

That was my first experience of one of the more important roles of the HoD – to be a listening ear whilst a staff member vents his or her anger or frustration. Commonly no interjection is required, just patience until the injustices are righted in the speaker's mind. He or she departs in a more relaxed mood and a potential glitch in the smooth running of the department has been avoided. Being the recipient of other people's unhappiness is, however, wearing and accumulative, and I found myself increasingly unable to deal sympathetically with what were usually minor problems.

Whatever the pressures, I did not break my prime rule – never lose your temper. When I have seen it happen to senior colleagues, I have invariably felt that it demeaned them. Other HoDs feel differently, one colleague told me that she used loss of temper, very rarely, as a shock tactic. She claimed spectacular results as grown men were rendered speechless.

Where does it all begin?

Most universities will have a formal description of how HoDs are chosen, for example, by departmental vote, by dictate of the Faculty Dean or even of the Vice-Chancellor (in exceptional control-freak cases). It is difficult to get at the truth – nobody would ever admit to wanting to be HoD, even though he or she has spent months priming the Dean about a willingness to sacrifice self for the common good. I suspect that there are three main methods for choosing HoDs:

The good soldier This is the acceptance that it is a moral obligation of the professoriate to be HoD at some stage and 'Regrettably, I am currently Buggins'. Skilful Deans will easily spot candidates with this in-built weakness.

Entrapment If Buggins refuses to do his or her turn, Buggins or some other candidate may be offered inducements, such as the continued employment of a post-doc or teaching assistant, or the promise of a full year's sabbatical at the end of the Headship period. Few universities seem to employ the obvious, but presumably *de trop*, method of making HoD allowance even moderately attractive.

Wishful thinking Some professors may see the Headship as a step towards greater administrative things, such as the Deanship or even *(sotto voce)* a Pro-Vice-Chancellorship. This is a high risk route, since there is little evidence that VCs consider being HoD as a useful training for anything much.

What do you have to do?

The recent expansion of the UK university system, without commensurate increase in funding, plus the seemingly endless round of research and teaching assessments, are necessitating significant changes in our working methods. All institutions are struggling to cope with these changes. Long-term planning, at all levels from the VC's office to the departmental, is increasingly difficult as we respond to external and internal demands for mission statements, student statistics or whatever, at, commonly, a few days or weeks notice. Last year, as we followed a major

internal audit by preparations for the HEFCE [Higher Education
Funding Council for England] Teaching Quality Assessment, a
colleague in Biological Sciences remarked to me that if you pull a
plant up often enough to look at its roots, it will die. I confessed
to feeling distinctly dehydrated around the radicles.

Against this background of continuing change, the role of
HoD has become increasingly confused. Some universities, including my own, have established committees to try to define
the requirements of the post. Almost all recommendations involve increased resources which are not available in financially
stringent times.

Part of the problem in producing a generalised description is
that the job is highly variable. Take, for example, the Heads of
Humanities and a Science department. They will require many
skills in common – the ability to manage and encourage staff,
the wisdom of Solomon in allocating teaching and administrative duties, the strength of character to represent the department at Faculty and higher levels, the patience to communicate
with central administration, a clear vision of the shape, development and research profile of their department, and the energy
to cope with the endless audits.

There are, though, many differences. The Humanities Head
will not normally have to manage (possibly large) technical
staff, a large resident population of research staff and students
and a complex and expensive suite of laboratories. The scale of
the job is different; the Head of a modestly sized Science department can easily have responsibility on a day-by-day basis for
150 people.

A major area of responsibility for the Science Head is safety.
New legislation is placing increasing burdens on the universities
and these are, necessarily, passed down to HoD level. I have
personal experience of being told, in most forcible terms, by an
officer of the Health and Safety Executive that I could be in
danger of litigation if certain improvements to our safety procedures were not carried out promptly. And this, I may say, in a
department which took safety issues extremely seriously.

Finally, there is normally a major difference in the financial
budgets. During several years of my Headship, our annual turnover exceeded £2.5 million, of which about half was external
income. There were hundreds, perhaps thousands (I didn't dare
check), of individual transactions, ranging from a box of test
tubes to spectrometers worth over £100k. Many institutions have
attempted some form of financial devolution, whereby departments take responsibility for the sound management of their

budgets. Whilst this affords a measure of flexibility and freedom in budgeting, it may also be a nightmare for someone who is not trained in financial management.

I looked forward rather eagerly to one HoD duty – attending Senate. At last a chance to find out how the university really works and perhaps to contribute in some small way. I sat beside a colleague with whom I had played cricket for the staff team some years previously. 'Rule number one, laddie. Always take some work to do at Senate; some letters to write, a book to review. Best place I know for a bit of peace and quiet.' Cynical, but regrettably true. Our Senate is simply too large to be truly effective. It reflects a major conundrum for universities; where is the balance between democratic representation and effective action? How flat can your administrative structure be when external pressures are most easily responded to by a pyramidal governance?

What makes a good HoD?

There is no template of a successful HoD. It is a complex function of personality and ambition. Some HoDs adopt the managerial approach, delegating every duty that can possibly be delegated but maintaining the role of ultimate arbiter. Others, in need perhaps of the moral high ground, get involved in every aspect of departmental business. Some drop all teaching, others carry heavy teaching loads. Some forgo personal research, others take the opportunity to pursue it more vigorously. Ultimately, the most important criterion of the success of a HoD is, 'Is the departmental prospectus in research and teaching being delivered?'

I think, though, that all good HoDs understand the need for constant communication with their staff. I found that if people were privy to how decisions were made and were allowed to comment on the process, they were usually willing to accept the decisions, no matter how unpalatable. It is also important that HoDs get their facts right, well in advance of meetings, whether at the individual or staff meeting level. It is, I suppose, a matter of simple trust.

It also helps to be a little street-wise, in the sense of understanding what motivates individuals and how they present themselves. I soon learned that when Dr X slid into my office, full of bonhomie and consideration for my welfare, he wanted money for something. Professor Y's jovial acquiescence to almost anything you put to him was followed by an almost total failure to do any task that he found uninteresting. To be able to predict someone's reaction to a given situation gives you the opportunity to be forearmed.

What do you do with 'difficult' academic staff?

This is one of the most contentious issues which a new HoD will have to face. There is a consensus that every department has some staff members who are unco-operative, who do not pull their weight, or who do not share in the current vision of the department's future. There is no consensus as to what constitutes the evidence for this view. The main culprit is the vagueness of the academic contract, which implicitly acknowledges that research creativity cannot be predicated on a nine to five basis and that *excellence* in teaching cannot be imparted.

If the HoD decides, therefore, to question formally the performance of a particular member of staff, he or she will be faced with a major stumbling block – where is the written statement of what, in detail, is expected or required? Confrontation on this basis is usually pointless. I preferred to try to get the best out of the staff involved, arguing that it is better to get 50% effort rather than virtually none from someone who is totally disenchanted. Future HoDs will have the advantage of more tightly written contracts for staff as universities address the problem of quantifiable performance indicators. They will still, however, have to acknowledge the fact that academic creativity cannot be manufactured and that every staff member will produce at different rates and in different styles.

Perks of the job?

Are there, indeed, any perks of the job? Of course there are:

- Being associated with the department's achieving a high research rating or an excellent in teaching.
- The pleasure of a colleague for whom you have successfully negotiated a promotion.
- The sense of repaying the system which has given you a job which, despite increasing problems, never fails to stimulate by giving you enormous scope for following teaching and research lines which are innovative and rewarding.

For me, one of the most enjoyable aspects of the job was in strengthening my interest in undergraduate teaching. It may have been partly age-related; my daughters were both at university and I thus had considerable empathy for the students. It was also a response to their enthusiasm, their camaraderie and their trust that you were delivering to them a course of which they could be proud. I would be less than strictly honest if I did not admit that spending an afternoon in a teaching laboratory was also a sweet way of getting away from the desk and admin chores.

One of the more taxing experiences of being Head was in having to deal with visiting students from northern European universities. They seemed to have a greater ability to see through what is termed in modern youth parlance, I believe, as bullshit, and were very efficient at seeing any gap between what was promised for a course and what was actually being delivered. One German student, in particular, was able to make me feel distinctly uncomfortable as I attempted to explain why Dr X's coursework still had not been marked and returned to them, or why students could not have access to the building after 6.00pm.

Handy hint for Heads

I would say that the main aim of the HoD should be to create and maintain for your colleagues a working environment which is stimulating, progressive, exciting, flexible, personally rewarding and *good-humoured*. I particularly stress the last point; get the atmosphere right and the department will look after itself.

(Macdonald 1997: 27–34)

Issues for administrators

As an administrator in a faculty or department, your role is likely to be either generalist (normally the senior administrative position) or specialist (supporting in-depth activities such as a teaching programme, marketing or industrial liaison). In either case there are attractions and limitations which are very different from those which apply to administrative work in the centre of the institution.

Attractions

1 The roles allow the administrator to operate at a distance from the more controlled atmosphere which tends to prevail in a central registry. This can be a liberating experience.
2 The roles place the administrator among the academic staff of the unit, bringing about a potentially much closer cooperative

relationship than is ever likely to be experienced between 'the centre' and an academic unit.

3 Close proximity enables a lot of time to be saved in the communication of messages and preparation of documents.

4 The administrator can become expert in the affairs of the unit. There are opportunities to immerse oneself in the subject matter so that one can effectively represent the unit with greater depth of understanding than is normally possible for an administrator who is physically remote.

5 The administrator may select a unit with which he or she may have an instinctive sympathy. While some professional administrators are versatile and able to adjust readily to different cultures, some flourish in a particular environment, for example in a science department, or in clinical and health-related units, or in a business school.

6 The 'immersion' factor is powerful. Hence an administrator for a teaching programme can become its organizer, financial manager, close adviser of its academic director, counsellor and confidant to its students, guardian of its assessment processes, supervisor and role model for its secretarial staff, sometimes its salesperson and chief recruiting agent. Alternatively, a faculty administrator may also fulfil the role of the Swiss Army knife, as a super-generalist dealing with finance, personnel, marketing, planning and policy, and facilities.

Limitations

1 An administrator appointed by an academic unit, even one seconded to it from the central administration, may be 'forgotten' by the centre and regarded as not 'one of us'.

2 The close proximity to academic staff has a potentially negative aspect if relationships with key people such as the dean, associate deans or heads of department become difficult. The relatively rapid turnover in the academic leadership positions creates the possibility that mutually beneficial relationships may disappear. It is, of course, more difficult to escape from an unfulfilling situation in an academic unit than in a central administration.

3 Being based at a remove from the centre means that special efforts have to be made to ensure that communications to and from the centre, which may include important but informal intelligence and political gossip, happen reliably. The value of an administrator to an academic unit is enhanced if he or she is well networked with administrative colleagues at the centre.

4 Although often able to write and talk cogently on behalf of a unit, the administrator may not always be given such credit by central officers who may expect to deal direct with senior academics. Such a stance can seem hypocritical when viewed in the context of senior officers' tendency to act – often appropriately – alongside or on behalf of senior academics such as pro-vice-chancellors and chairs of committee.
5 Becoming immersed in the business of any one unit for a long period can limit career prospects, unless the subject area is sufficiently well developed to offer career openings nationally or internationally. Certainly an ignorance of central institutional issues is a disadvantage.

The following advertisements for faculty-based administrative jobs all appeared simultaneously, in March 1998. They represent a range of universities – Northumbria, Cambridge and London – and a range of subjects. Salaries range between £21,016 and £31,269 per annum. They show a considerable overlap of qualities sought. Readers may find it amusing to identify the university from the amended text.

Example A

A flexible person with first-class organizational skills is required to manage the general administration of this key department within an exciting and dynamic environment.

You will work closely with the Professor and will deal with the organization of teaching, budgets and accounts, staff recruitment and appraisal, management of research information and literature and publicity.

You will be educated to degree level or equivalent, and must have proven experience of managing office routines, including staff supervision. Excellent WP and database skills, and well-developed written and interpersonal communication skills, are also essential. A background in Higher Education would be an advantage.

(*Guardian*, 31 March 1998)

Example B

We are looking for a pro-active, enthusiastic and experienced administrator who has excellent people management and leadership skills to deliver a high quality administrative support service.

Responsible jointly to the Dean and the University's Registrar, you will be involved with student, programme and research administration and with ensuring support for management, particularly in academic and resource planning and the quality of teaching and research activities. Part of the role is also to work with the Registrar as part of a wider team in developing and enhancing University-wide academic support processes and procedures.

This is a busy and high profile role in which supporting and leading the administrative teams will be a key function. Excellent interpersonal skills and a commitment to team working on a self managed basis in a changing environment are essential. Qualified to degree level, you should have sound administrative skills and understanding of how IT can support academic administration and management. Previous experience in Higher Education would be helpful.

(The Times Higher, 27 March 1998)

Example C

The University is seeking to appoint a senior administrator from 1 October 1998, to take up the office of Secretary of the Department and to act also as Secretary of the Faculty Board, when the current job holder retires at the end of October.

The main responsibilities of this role are to manage the administrative functions of this large and complex department, with delegated authority from the Head of Department for the management of the Department's resources. The Secretary will also advise and support the Head of Department, Chairman of the Faculty Board and other academic staff on administrative and financial matters. In addition to overseeing the administration of the Department, the Secretary will carry out many of the day-to-day administrative tasks and will, therefore, need to develop detailed knowledge of all aspects of the Department's activities.

Candidates should be educated to degree level. They must possess good communication and management skills and be flexible and well organized. Previous relevant experience in a senior administrative post is essential, preferably in a higher education establishment with a research grant portfolio.

(The Times Higher, 27 March 1998)

Example A: Institute of Psychiatry, University of London
Example B: Faculty of Social Sciences, University of Northumbria at Newcastle
Example C: Department of Clinical Veterinary Medicine, University of Cambridge

6

BUSINESS ISSUES

What are the alternatives for dealing with everyday business? The advantages of dealing with them at central or, alternatively, at unit level are distinctly different. For each activity, there may be different – and shifting – levels of aggregation at which business should be handled.

A list of business issues would be as long as the entire set of activities undertaken by HEIs. Let us pay attention only to major areas such as finance, personnel, marketing, student recruitment, facilities, and quality.

Finance

The area ranges from major institutional issues such as new building projects, investment and borrowing decisions, through the setting of budgets, to monitoring procedures and travelling expense claims. A traditional view of finance in higher education was to treat it as a centrally determined set of activities managed by qualified accountants. It was not likely to be transparent to departments who were allocated academic and other staff positions according to the number of funded students they taught and other, possibly historical, factors and required to operate within set budgets. Monitoring tended to concentrate heavily on control of expenditure rather than on generation of income. Departmental allocations were affected also by 'fudge factors' such as varying the units of resource for teaching students and by assertions and beliefs about the quality of research undertaken and about the level of operating costs thought to be appropriate. On this model, budget-setting was a highly political process based on the premise that there was a cake of defined size to be sliced up. At powerful committees, the winners were those who shouted loudest and most eloquently. Units needed to monitor their expenditure, perhaps running a pencil and paper system alongside the computerized printouts which the Finance Office issued for each month approximately two weeks after the end of the month concerned. For a science department with many research grants, the amount of monitoring and sums involved could be extremely large, whereas for a typical humanities department 90 per cent of expenditure would be on salaries at predetermined levels.

Since the late 1970s, several trends have caused major changes to occur in the financial management of HEIs. These include the expansion of student numbers, the reduction in the unit of resource (that is funding per student) accompanied by the need for savings combined with pressure to generate additional income.

The expansion of the system created pressure to devolve more responsibility to the level of the cost centre on the assumption that the best financial outcomes are likely to be achieved by those closest to buying and selling decisions. The trend towards devolution was accelerated by an awareness that many commercial enterprises were cutting costs at head office level and increasing budgetary power and incentives at the level of subsidiaries. Among the changes which have occurred alongside new financial regimes are a substantial increase in international students who pay fees at, or close to, the full cost of their education, increases in taught courses and consultancy for businesses which also pay at full-cost levels, and more efficient teaching methods which have increased the ratio of students to staff.

Greater awareness of financial issues has produced not only undoubted benefits but also some unproductive behaviour. Setting budgets has always been an intensely political process, perhaps shown most clearly in 'historic cost' situations in which budget-holders essentially agreed to take a rise at the level of inflation without debating actual needs – a case of holding on to gains won in previous years. At least such a process has the merit of minimizing the amount of senior staff time diverted to the activity of budget-setting.

Game-playing has always been indulged in, and some institutions have suffered as a result of setting rules which encouraged inappropriate behaviour. In the old public sector system, a unit which underspent its budget was likely to be severely criticized and penalized: it might be seen as failing in its duty to deliver an agreed service, perhaps accused of dishonesty the previous year in arguing for more funds than it required, and penalized by having its new year's budget pegged at the level of the previous year's actual expenditure. If the unit had also earned extra income, the managers of the system could be equally critical. The behaviour encouraged by such a process was that budget-holders were conservative in their spending, in order to maintain a contingency, and in their generation of income, in order to avoid being placed under obligations to generate yet more income. Towards the year-end, they would spend energetically, up to the level of their budget. In some cases they even asked suppliers to present them with advance invoices so that they could be seen to have spent the money, thus damaging their organization's cash-flow situation. As a result, the organization understood little, if anything, about its true potential to save money or make money – all because its procedures had encouraged budget-holders to obscure the process by playing games. There is evidence that in all too many organizations this kind of situation still prevails. However, it is rational in that it provides quite a high level of stability, particularly if there are tight controls to avoid overspending.

What better alternatives are there? They can all be summarized in one word – incentives. If the organization wishes to improve its business position, one way to do so is to encourage some or all of its units to generate a surplus. That money can then be reinvested to enable the organization to improve its services. For a start, in-year flexibility is desirable. It may be 18 months from the approval of a budget to the end of the budget year in question. All kinds of problems and opportunities will arise, presenting the budget manager with situations in which he or she may have to overspend in one activity but could cope by setting it against underspending in other activities. This is known as virement and, on a known and controlled basis, it is a desirable feature of a budget monitoring system. Additional income might become available but, in order to generate it, extra expenditure might have to be incurred. An organization which refuses to allow a budget-holder to exceed an expenditure budget by £10,000 in order to better the income budget by £20,000 might be regarded as foolish, but such cases have arisen, particularly if the unit concerned has a credibility problem (will it really deliver the £20,000?).

At the approach of the year-end, will the unit see its £10,000 surplus disappear into a black hole in the accounts? Will its own accounts simply be reset to zero for the start of the new year? If so, the unit may well conclude that there are no incentives to save if it cannot spend or reinvest at least part of the surplus which it has earned – perhaps at high personal cost in terms of hard work and long hours.

A lack of financial incentives can disable a whole institution. For example, if departments are forced to concentrate on living within expenditure budgets which are disconnected from the income they generate, their behaviour will tend to become unenterprising or risk averse. Even where the system allows them to earn money, for example by teaching on programmes elsewhere in the institution, that money will not motivate them if it cannot be spent. The head of a department in this situation complained of being 'paid in roubles'. The same department would be acting irrationally if it pressed forward with its plan to create and market a potentially lucrative postgraduate programme, for it would thereby divert itself from its research and other teaching commitments and exceed its budgets in order to generate income which it would not be allowed to spend. This is an illustration of how 'prudence' at the centre can cost the institution dear in terms of income forgone. The lack of suitable incentives can hit home even harder at the individual level as this facetious little parable shows.

Box 6.1 A parable about a lack of incentives

One day, an unscrupulous academic discovered how to make perfect £20 notes. This was a rather unpleasant process and he could only make about five notes/hour. Materials for each note cost him £3 which had to be paid in advance before he could make any notes so his net profit on each note was £17. He worked out that he therefore could make about £85/hour (not much for an accountant maybe but it was considerably more than he earned as an academic).

He dreamed of holidays in Jamaica with dusky maidens serving his every need.

However, a greedy administrator who had control over his money told him that he would have to pay a tax of £5 for every note that he made, that he would have to give £5 to his neighbours who preferred to read books rather than make money and that he would have to save £5 for the future (though it wasn't clear that he would ever be allowed to spend it and spending on dusky maidens was expressly forbidden). He thought about this for a while and worked out that this left him with £2 per note and a net hourly rate of £10/hour.

Even academics are paid more than this so he decided that this money-making lark wasn't worth the bother. So he went back to reading books.

(Professor Ian Sommerville, Computing Department, Lancaster University)

Nevertheless, central financial managers may be failing in their duty if they simply replace controls with incentives. Some units will perform worse than budget and where can the organization make up for the shortfall if compensating surpluses are ring-fenced for the use of those who earned them? In order to get the best out of incentives, controls must be in place. For example, the centre must be able to intervene to prevent further additional expenditure in a unit when it becomes clear to all that good money is being thrown after bad in a project which is not proving to be the expected business success. There have to be negative incentives too, such as fear of the consequences of failure. If units are rewarded by being allowed to carry forward a surplus for later use, then it is equitable that those who end the year with a deficit should be punished by being required to work it off during the following year. Normally, the organization must actually implement such a system, otherwise the surpluses and deficits are on paper only, and incentives disappear. If the sums become extremely large, then the 'wealthy' will run out of sensible or equitable uses for the money, the 'poor' will fall so far into debt that they lose the commitment to turn things around. There are organizations which have in effect been forced to spend units' surpluses on operating costs, leaving the units with a paper credit, and to write off huge accumulated deficits in other units. Again incentives break down and a lot of ill feeling is generated. A well managed financial system should enable an organization to reap benefits from surplus-generators, by contracting with them to share the surplus so that other units may receive subsidies on a properly evaluated and planned basis. It should also prompt action in the case of chronic loss-making. The reasons must be understood and perhaps the institution will conclude that it cannot make the activity pay and must close down part or all of it. If something can be salvaged and might prosper, a recovery plan – regularly and vigorously monitored by the centre – could be put in place.

Some well-developed faculties have made agreements with their parent HEI about devolved responsibilities which can enable the faculty concerned to move quickly in making appointments. Naturally such arrangements can apply only where the institution has confidence in the quality of management in each faculty.

The following is an actual agreement which has been in place for 13 years in a UK university:

Devolution of responsibility for resource allocation

Conditions of devolution of responsibility for resources to the Faculties.

1 The Finance Committee will remain responsible to the Court for all aspects of the University budget.

2 The Finance Committee will identify and notify to the University Management Group as early as possible in each financial year the total amount available for allocation across all the Faculties and resource groups. The University Management Group will, on receipt of notification of the total amount, agree to recommend an amount to be allocated by Finance Committee to each of the Faculties and resource groups and to the University Management Group's own contingency fund. The Finance Committee will then resolve, modify, or refer back the recommended allocations. The financial performance of each resource group will be subject to monitoring by Finance Committee.

3 The University Management Group will maintain a five year rolling plan which will be reviewed annually in consultation with Faculties and which will form a background to resource allocation decisions at all levels.

The performance of each Faculty will be subject to monitoring by the University Management Group against current planning and policy.

4 The resource groups will consist of the Faculties and other groups as may be determined by Court from time to time after receiving the advice of the University Management Group.

5 The Finance Committee will allocate the faculty budget to the Faculty budget holder who shall be personally responsible to the Finance Committee for the allocation of resources within the Faculty and for effective budget control under financial rules of practice laid down by Finance Committee.

6 Each Faculty will be required to establish a resource committee which will have the right to be kept fully informed and the responsibility to advise the Dean on resource management. The resource committee's approval to the annual estimates and budget of the Faculty will be required.

7 The Dean of the Faculty will be the budget holder and will be required to seek and receive the advice of a faculty resource committee.

8 The resource committee will be constituted with a membership determined by Court on advice from the University Management Group. In the first instance, the resource committees will consist of:

The Dean (Chairman)
The Vice-Dean and Associate Deans

Heads of Departments in the Faculty
Two members nominated by the Faculty Board of Studies

9 Each Faculty will have a 'Faculty Officer' who will be secretary to the Board of Studies and the resource committee, and will be directly responsible to the Dean in operational terms and to the Registrar and Director of Finance in terms of professional practice.

10 The heads of departments and of units within each Faculty to which resources are allocated in the faculty budget will be responsible to the Dean for the allocation of resources within the department or unit and for effective budget control under financial rules of practice laid down by Finance Committee. Heads of departments and of units who consider that they have been unfairly treated by the Faculty, may appeal by a stated case to the University Management Group.

11 The authority to appoint staff, including academic staff, from within resources available to the Faculty will be vested in the Dean subject to:

- the advance approval of the faculty resource committee in each case,
- the advance approval of the University Management Group in the case of professorial appointments,
- the observance of Ordinances or other procedures that may apply in each case.

12 Visiting and honorary appointments will be made on the authority of the Dean subject to the advice of the Faculty resource committee, provided that details of all such appointments are made available to the Personnel Office before the appointment is effective and that in the case of professorial appointments, details are made available to the University Management Group.

13 Where it is decided that a post which is being vacated should not or cannot be filled without a void, the actual salary which is budgeted for, but not paid, shall be credited to the Faculty and shall not be withheld by the University.

14 Advertising, interview and resettlement expenses budgets will continue to be accessible to Deans from the Personnel Office but, in the case of advertising and interviews, it will be open to Deans to supplement that source from faculty funds.

15 The post of Faculty Officer will be financed under the administration budget of the University. All other administrative, clerical and support costs required to support the Dean,

shall be financed from the faculty budget (subject to initial transfer arrangements).

16 The allocation of space will remain in the immediate future, a responsibility of the Accommodation Sub-Committee. However, it is expected that Deans will be kept informed of all transactions relevant to their respective Faculties and will be consulted whenever appropriate.

17 The allocation of funds earmarked for expenditure on scientific equipment and furnishing, will continue to be the responsibility of the Equipment and Furniture Committee. The Committee will be expected to make block allocations available to each Dean on the basis of agreed criteria. The Committee will retain an amount sufficient on the basis of experience to respond to the needs of non-faculty areas for exceptional requirements.

There are other interesting choices to be made at the operating level. A centralized system should provide budget-holders with comprehensible accounts as well as fulfilling the institution's obligations to maintain records. In particular, the system should be on-line so that recognized users can access it at any time, not just waiting for a monthly report. Large-scale purchases will need commitment accounting to be a feature of the system so that the costs they have incurred by placing orders are reflected promptly in the accounts, rather than awaiting the arrival and authorization of an invoice. At the year-end and at any important review stages during the year, mistaken decisions can be made in the absence of a commitment-accounting system. Ideally, the central record system and its communications with budget-holders and purchasers in the units should be so good that the units do not need to maintain parallel records. Any significant weakness in the central system will undermine units' confidence in it and lead them to incur considerable costs in salaries, staff training and equipment to perform what is, in part at least, a duplicate function. Devolution – otherwise welcomed – can bring with it a requirement to process all one's own purchase orders, to enter them on to the computer system, to print off the periodic accounts for local monitoring, to chase one's own debtors, to respond to creditors chasing *their* invoices and, of course, to maintain one's own accounts which may or may not be derived from the central record system. One typical feature of such devolution is the export of functions from the centre to the units which have to incur additional costs while savings are made at the centre.

Nevertheless, HEIs have tended to fall short of gaining the full benefits of devolution. For reasons of control, units are not normally permitted to issue cheques against the expenditure they have incurred. They have to authorize on sheets of paper, enter them on the system, and send them to a central payments office which, subject to the institution's current policy on payments and pressures relating to cash-flow, subsequently issues a cheque. Units are not normally happy to have to expend resource in processing the payment, fielding the incoming phone calls from creditors and contributing their share of the cost of central overheads which in this case is essentially a duplicate function. Why not save resources by authorizing approved units to print cheques on behalf of the institution, subject to some protocols to ensure that mistakes are not made?

Before deciding upon the principles and operational features of the financial system, the institution should give further thought to incentives, other than the issue of whether units may vire expenditure within a budget, negotiate changes to budgets within year and retain some or all of their surplus. Within a unit, the choice of financial regime has far-reaching consequences. Most heads of department and programmes directors prefer to work to a budget, particularly if it is one to which they have contributed some ideas rather than having it imposed on them or having their draft budget savaged. It becomes an additional challenge and source of pride to operate effectively and also within a budget. However, in some cases, the budget-holder looks to an administrator to transact purchases and do most of the detailed reconciliation work. This is particularly the case if the information system is deficient or difficult to comprehend. The unit faces at its level the same choice as the institution: what incentives and penalties will attach to the level of budget performance? Perhaps the worst outcomes are that the successful are punished by being denied access to their surplus and by suffering adverse adjustments (raised income targets, lowered expenditure allowances) the following year; and that failure is rewarded by more generous allocations, perhaps taken from the surplus generated by others; that in-year control is either absent so that problems are not detected and solved, or so rigorous that people's time is dominated by demands to account for minor variances.

Some public sector bodies have in the past been guilty of setting budgets on behalf of units, giving them no understanding of how or why the budgets were arrived at. This helped to produce a perception that there was something unreal and mysterious about finance. There was nothing to be gained by delving into financial matters and no incentive to act to improve cash-flow or obtain better value for money. For example, the department which takes the easy path of phoning its friendly supplier of test-tubes or stationery when it needs to restock is in danger of failing to notice that the supplier may be taking advantage by raising prices beyond those of rival suppliers and of failing to negotiate discounts and save staff time by ordering in bulk and less frequently. The department that invoices employers or students who attend its external courses may be content to delay the process for three months. As long as enough invoices are sent out by 31 July and are credited to the current financial year, the budget target will be met. And yet if payment had been obtained three months earlier, the institution could have used the money productively by investing it at interest or reducing its need to borrow at interest. Finance officers are sometimes guilty of failing to make these points, which are obvious to them, known to budget-holders. Whether and how the benefits of good business practice should be shared with units, rather than retained at the centre, are questions which should be live issues.

'Old-style' behaviour within a unit could produce problems if earnings increased within a financially 'unreal' atmosphere. Windfall grants or external contracts can generate extra income, sometimes at a level which is high in relation to the unit's accustomed level of discretionary expenditure. Without financial awareness or experience of obtaining value for money, budget-holders could simply misuse the money, perhaps lavishing it on unnecessary expenditure or using it to take on staff to whom commitments, including redundancy payments, may outlive the duration of the income.

However, the experience of the majority is very different. Once budgets begin to be set within a unit, a competitive atmosphere tends to arise. The challenge for heads is to make that competition creative. Some activities, particularly those which are new or experimental, will not be capable of covering all their costs, at least initially. The unit needs a strategy to guide its decisions about which activities can be permitted and what targets will apply to them. Other budget-holders, whose surplus provides the cross-subsidy, need have no complaints provided that the beneficiaries manage their affairs competently.

Commercial organizations are familiar with the notion of investing in loss-making activities: there is nothing inherently unbusinesslike about them since they may be performing a service which is essential for the commercially successful activities or developing an activity which may become surplus generating in the future. Competition between budget-holders is normally healthy if it concerns the provision of services, the recruitment of students or the generation of surplus, subject to maintaining standards. Competition is less healthy at the budget-setting stage (the grab for resources) and within year if it encourages narrow-minded and short-term thinking. Budget-holders may waste their energies and produce decisions which may be against the interests of the unit as a whole. For example, they may engage in bitter arguments about which other budget-holders should share with them the cost of an advertisement and write text which reflects no credit on other activities or finally decide not to advertise at all. They may decide to teach their students in dilapidated rooms which the institution provides free of charge rather than pay an internal charge of £50 for a room which is designed for the needs of the class. Suboptimal decisions of this kind are not necessarily the fault of short-sighted budget-holders; they may be rational responses to a regime which is unduly strict about expenditure or which declares financial outcome in the current year to be the most important performance indicator.

Whether at the centre or within a unit, decisions have to be taken about expenditure on activities which do, or may, not generate income. Just as commercial organizations have reduced their overheads by reducing staff in head office, so HEIs have become more aware of the need for maximum effectiveness in corporate, service or administrative functions. Declining units of resource have made it imperative that a large percentage of income should be retained by the units which generate it. Hence central services are, properly, under pressure to demonstrate that they provide good value for money. Directly or indirectly, they should add value to the income-generating units, making their priority tasks easier to achieve. When those units are in effect being taxed so that central services can run, it is not surprising that they can be critical of the quality of service provided. They have a right to expect that central services will provide advice, undertake some tasks on their behalf and certainly not obstruct them or dump low value-added tasks upon them.

Those issues have a familiar ring in the 'them' and 'us' world of central administrations and academic units. However, the same issues, scaled down, often apply at the level of the unit. It, too, has to decide how to handle its administrative load (for instance choosing between the use of academic staff or professional administrators) and what functions to require from its administrative service. In a situation which is *budget-informed*, as it should be, the costs and benefits of each service and each academic activity can be calculated, or at least assessed. In a situation which is *budget-driven*, there is a danger that the bids of income-earning groups will be met in full, while the non-earning functions are starved of resources. Those earning large sums are often not asked hard questions about their expenditure budget. It could be foolishly short-sighted, for example, to approve full-cost teaching programmes spending on glossy brochures, modern but little-used teaching aids, and generous hospitality while making minimal provision for managing quality assurance processes at the levels of the programme and the unit as a whole.

A study of financial devolution (Thomas 1997) echoes some of these concerns, and others, about devolution in higher education. For example, the dangers of encouraging entrepreneurial behaviour at the local level without a sound management information system and of allowing free rein to income-generating groups which might operate in a self-interested manner and without the requisite management skills are outlined. There is evidence that devolution to too low a level (that is departments or subgroups) can cause a decline in effectiveness at the level of the faculty or school where, it is arguable, greater benefits of devolution may be available. As is suggested elsewhere in this book, it may be that it is at the level of such larger units that operations will prove most cost-effective and most collegial and congenial to the staff employed in academic units. Unless there is an excellent central information system, responsible units will have to invest in their own staffing and staff training for financial transactions. This non-added-value activity is not likely to make sense unless the financial enterprise concerned is of substantial size.

However, it would be unfortunate if the limitations of devolving responsibility to the lowest operating levels were taken as evidence to centralize and avoid any form of meaningful devolution. Tight control at the centre cannot be informed by an understanding of the various markets in which the institution operates and the accompanying tendency to minimize expenditure as the main route to financial health can strangle the academic energies on which the institution depends. The task for those at the centre is to set out sufficient incentives to motivate the academic entrepreneurs while retaining sufficient control and funding to solve the financial problems which inevitably arise somewhere in the organization. Even more important, central services have an obligation, which some have failed to deliver, to provide information systems which are accurate, timely and usable by the academic units as well as by the management accountants.

Personnel

HEIs' expenditure on salaries is relatively heavy and inflexible: payroll is by far the largest item in most departments' budget and, what is more, most staff work on permanent or protected contracts. Flexibility, in the sense of achieving high levels of turnover, is attainable only in the medium to long term.

This major investment in staff is not always reflected in policy and practice. For example, the percentage of budget directed to developing the staff is typically low by industrial standards. The personnel function within HEIs has become loaded with more bureaucratic functions arising from the need to conform to changes in the law or in 'good employment practice', HEIs taking the view that they cannot afford to be associated with anything which might be perceived as unfair treatment of current or prospective staff. Important decisions – such as which staff positions will be filled, who will be recruited, who will be promoted or otherwise rewarded, and how staff are guided and developed – are taken by academic units subject to the approval of central committees. Personnel is cast in the role of watchdog, attempting to ensure that academic staff do not cut corners, or otherwise breach equal opportunities guidelines. It must also carry out a plethora of other functions which are not normally delegated to the level of academic units. These include placing advertisements, responding to enquiries, processing applications, taking up references, issuing offer letters, the renewal and termination of contracts, managing the regradings and promotions processes and running the management information systems which are supposed to capture all the data. On a less routine level, they also become involved in normally protracted special cases, such as disciplinary and grievance, and issues arising from the reorganization of departments and faculties.

Additional burdens placed on central personnel offices make it rational for more functions to be delegated to academic units. With the caveat that only the institution is empowered to offer, extend or terminate contracts of employment, nevertheless a well-organized faculty office can handle a high volume of routine personnel matters.

The local office, which knows the people, is in principle capable of a wide range of functions – taking up references, communicating with shortlisted candidates before and after interview, conducting appraisals, reviewing and renewing (or not renewing) fixed-term contracts, offering part-time or honorary appointments, implementing changes to job descriptions or hours of work. One is tempted to add fixing levels of salary at appointment and rewards, whether performance related or not. At or well short of that point, many institutions would draw a line and insist upon central control of decisions, fearing the consequences of units' autonomous decisions. Clearly there is a point which is 'too far' in personnel administration, particularly if there are any doubts about the objectivity of decision making or the quality of organization at the unit level. However, many institutions have been unduly cautious about delegation of responsibility and so continue to process routine matters twice, first in the form of proposals from the unit which are ratified and reprocessed by central personnel. In addition to costly duplication, the second layer incurs extra costs in delays and misunderstandings.

However, from time to time difficult matters requiring specialist knowledge will arise or, as in the case of obtaining work permits, the appropriate level of aggregation is likely to be one central office. Therefore there will be a continuing need for a personnel 'head office'.

All central personnel officers should, at minimum, ensure that they have a reliable database to which units can refer when they wish to check duration of contracts, retirement dates or levels of payment. Nothing is more irritating for an academic unit than to conclude that it can get an accurate database only by creating its own or to be asked to take action when the request is triggered by false information held on a central record.

Central functions cannot be expected to provide more than a framework for staff development. The units themselves are in effect responsible for their own selection decisions, and should therefore aim to maximize the likelihood of a mutually fulfilling relationship with their staff. Hence their own induction, mentoring, development and appraisal processes should overlay whatever structure is set up centrally.

Academic pay has fallen steadily behind that in comparable professions, but it is not the case that all has been silent despair. Some institutions have created performance-related pay schemes, the flexibility to appoint at levels reflecting the job market in the subject and to award accelerated or additional increments has increased, and mobility has been enhanced by the 'transfer market' associated with the RAE. In the latter case, there have been many instances of staff moving from one institution to another, particularly within a region. This phenomenon seems to suggest a willingness to shift professional allegiance without necessarily disturbing personal and family arrangements.

Professorial pay has tended to become more variable, increasingly reflecting market factors rather than expectations based upon years of service combined with dates of promotion. In so far as actual pay differs from the predictable working out of incremental progression on particular scales, there is an issue about power and influence. Does the vice-chancellor, or whatever central body recommends non-standard rewards, consult the head of the academic unit concerned? If not, the position of the dean is seriously undermined, particularly as decisions affect the ability to attract new staff and the perceived fairness of relative salaries. To be properly empowered and accountable, the head of the unit needs to be able to operate with considerable, but agreed, degrees of freedom. Major issues of morale and motivation are at stake.

Additional earnings by academic staff

Many departments face other issues about levels of payment. It is increasingly possible for academic staff to earn additional, overtime, payments for contributing to surplus-generating activities. Most institutions have a code of practice to cover such cases and they tend to have in common a requirement that, prior to undertaking such work, the individual must inform a senior member of the institution – normally at least the head of department. The sensitivities involved are such that a detailed code of practice is desirable. Although the issues are more likely to arise in professional schools than elsewhere, there is always the potential for them to do so. Consider this minefield:

1 *Private consultancy* Working in his or her own time, a lecturer earns money by advising another organization and is paid directly by that organization. Most 'home' institutions will be at pains to ensure that in such a case, it is made clear that the lecturer does not represent the institution and does not use departmental stationery and support staffing. The home institution is not responsible for the quality of the work delivered.

Problems include the danger that, if set working hours are not specified, it will be difficult for a head of department to be satisfied that the work is indeed an overtime job. If it is carried out in working time, then arguably the lecturer is being paid twice over and it could be said that public funds are being misused. Hence the desirability of establishing that all such work is in addition to a normal, full load of duties.

The lecturer may take the view that he or she is entitled to receive 100 per cent of the income and may reflect that the matter might have been concealed without anyone knowing about it. However, is it fair that the institution which bears the cost of his or her overheads receives nothing? Also, it is arguable that, without the status which derives from the professional position, the work might not have been offered.

If the work proves mutually satisfactory, it may be repeated and extended. At what point does a real conflict of interest develop and when will the department begin to notice the lecturer's increasing absences and declining publications?

And yet . . . the work may be highly desirable. It might provide the practical complement to the lecturer's research, enrich his or her teaching with up-to-date, real-world examples and provide motivation to stay with the institution when otherwise a static salary might encourage the thought of alternative employment. It might also make a favourable impression on the client and so enhance the reputation of the whole institution.

2 *Additional earnings within the department* If work expands beyond the accustomed capacity of the existing staff, and new appointments cannot be made within the required time-scale, then the unit may have to decide between buying in teaching from elsewhere or paying its own staff overtime to carry it out.

Problems here include the obvious one that the additional activity must generate sufficient income to make extra expenditure possible, unless of course the department's situation is so dire that it must take on extra work to meet its budget. Diverting any money to individuals is then out of the question, however hard they are working. A more probable danger is that the work is seen as a moral obligation on the department without generating more than very basic income.

If it is full-cost work, then it is likely to be high profile because of the expectations of the students or clients. In that case, the institution might lose face by being seen to farm out the teaching to another institution (indeed, the terms of the contract might rule out such subcontracting). An exception would be the use of acknowledged experts from outside whose involvement would be seen as adding, not reducing, value for money. While it may be possible on one occasion to persuade staff to take on the extra work at a probable cost to their research and private life, it is not a sound principle on a repeated or established basis. A short course might appropriately be resourced by teachers earning overtime, but a wrong message may be given by handling a whole degree programme in that way. The programme might become seen as non-core and hence less important than other work when it is possible that the development of such activity should be the new main-stream priority.

While there are virtues – as in external consultancy – in offering opportunities for additional earnings, issues of fairness and balance soon arise. How are staff selected to undertake the work? Are they all rewarded on a comparable basis and does that matter? At which point does the work become so substantial that core duties can no longer be fulfilled? Is it acceptable that a lecturer in one faculty can benefit from 'market forces' whereas an equally gifted teacher in another faculty gains no such opportunity?

Certainly, it is arguable that – unlike the case of consultancy contracts won by a lecturer – the work is 'delivered to the door' without
the need for effort on the part of the teacher. In such a case, it is not
appropriate for payment to be made at the highest level countenanced
by the institution, even though that is what the teacher may claim!

The use of variable levels of payment has caused problems in
departments in which traditional assumptions also operate. For
example, the belief that all should be treated equally has caused
programmes to pay out excessively large sums when they assume
that the bought-in lecturer from the local college or, indeed, their
own junior lecturer, should be paid at the same rate as a leading
external consultant or academic.

3 *Categories of staff* Academic staff may be paid overtime and so
may secretarial and manual staff. Traditionally, HEIs held to a
view that professional staff (academics being mysteriously exempt
from the category for this purpose!) should do the job expected
of them without expectation of payment for overtime. Hence,
administrators and accountants in higher education have found
themselves excluded from reward despite having made essential
contributions to the delivery of a commercial project. It is understandable that HEIs literally cannot afford to introduce unpredict-
able liabilities into their salaries bill, and yet greater flexibility in
this respect would improve the morale of the regularly overworked.

Unequal treatment has been defended on the grounds that the
'academic entrepreneur' is a known phenomenon. Making money
through intellectual property is of course a different matter. When
it comes to running full-cost teaching programmes and other commercial projects, the entrepreneurial effort is as likely to have come
from the administrator as from the academic who may be doing no
more than turning up to deliver a teaching slot, then departing.

The leaders of the academic unit have to make difficult, balanced judgements about how best to motivate and reward their
people under conditions in which insufficient rewards are available. They are likely to have to bargain with the guardians of
institutional procedures in order to maintain incentives for the
unit to develop and succeed. Sometimes the central guardians do
not seem to appreciate that development and success in the units
is a precondition for *institutional* development and success.

Staff development

It is a commonplace that HEIs' most important resource is their
people, yet they have gone about developing their staff in tentative

and ineffective ways. Either because the culture has decreed that a central office should not attempt to dictate practice to academic departments or because those offices are short of resources or ideas, most staff development is left to occur at department level. Even required practices such as regular appraisal may not be subject to checking, that is, has it happened and with what implications for staff development? Some institutions make a virtue of delegating development but they must know that in some departments nothing happens unless it is on the initiative of individual staff. There has been a degree of justified scepticism about being 'sent on courses', and too many examples of individuals having experienced programmes of little benefit to them. This has led to the retort, 'Staff development? I haven't got time for that.' Fortunately, staff developers have pointed out the many forms of development activity which do not entail going on a course. Much constructive development activity does undoubtedly occur, for example, the mentoring and guidance of new lecturers to help them to produce articles worthy of publication and to improve their teaching.

We are almost certainly entering an era when neglecting staff development will be seen as bad management. Managements which do not check up to ensure that all departments are following at least the basic elements of the institution's staff development policy, do not publicize external or in-house training opportunities, or fail to allocate anything more than derisory sums in their central and faculty budgets, will be open to increasingly fierce criticism from quality assurance bodies. Specific pressures such as required training for lecturers and graduate teaching assistants and the explicit linking of staff development to organizational objectives, as under Investors in People, are providing extra impetus to improve the effectiveness of staff development.

Very important, and often forgotten, is the monitoring of staff development activities to gauge their effectiveness. If this is not done, it is easy to slip into an assumption that spending some money or attending a workshop has solved a problem. Evaluating development activities can be built into appraisal and also informs the unit about the desirability of those activities for other staff. Evaluation of training and development is another important plank of Investors in People.

The field of staff development is one which leaders of academic units should study to ensure that central provision meets local needs. The unit may need to create tailored programmes for its own staff, either negotiating an appropriate share of the central budget or supplementing it by setting aside some of its own funds.

Marketing   ■

There are sound reasons for adhering to a central marketing and promotion strategy. Those who have been responsible for marketing or public relations share a view that once departments or individuals have direct, unmanaged contact with the media, mixed messages will result. The illusion of a unified institution will be shattered and damaging implications may be read into the actions or words of individual staff. All messages should be overlaid by an understanding of the full context which can be guaranteed only through an informed liaison person at the centre. Indeed there are examples of effective central marketing, such as undergraduate recruitment by some post-1992 universities and the consistent use of a visual identity by many institutions.

If the institution has a clear strategy, perhaps to differentiate itself sharply from two others within the same city by emphasizing key characteristics (shall we say these are access and regional partnerships?) then the basis of its marketing plan is already determined. It will beam messages through local and regional media, including radio and television as well as newspapers, and will approach regional colleges, companies, clubs, societies and alumni. Dealing with national and international media will be correspondingly less important to it.

Will this situation be satisfactory to the constituent academic units? If they have participated in the formation of the strategy and share fully in it, then the answer should be, 'Yes'. The units' programmes and individuals will be living examples of the activities which the institution stands for and wishes to promote. Hence they will operate through central publicity and marketing offices with little, if any, need to resource their own marketing activities. Even small-scale activities such as publishing a departmental brochure will probably involve them only in providing text which will then be cast into institutional house-style, designed and printed through a central office. When a lecturer designs a new form of industrial robot, the story will be developed and promoted to the media through the central office which will emphasize again the institution's contribution to the regional economy.

Why are marketing situations rarely so simple and satisfactory? In the expanded and more diverse world of modern higher education, an academic unit is quite unlikely to be in a position to share much of its strategy with that of other units. At the very least, it will have distinct 'publics' which it needs to reach. A set of lively, proactive faculties will tend to create a 'multiversity' culture, sharing certain key assumptions provided that central processes have been sufficiently well managed to identify and agree them. The implications for marketing are significant. A sceptic might question the need for consistency in marketing. Why not let communications reflect the truth, that the institution is diverse? However, for the sake of avoiding duplication and maximizing value for money, some planning and collective effort seems rational. The question is whether the appropriate level of that collective effort is the institution, the faculty, or the department.

It is noteworthy that the more successful marketing communications tend to promote coherent, rather than diverse, services. At the postgraduate level, effective institution-wide messages are rare because of the diverse nature of the products. Significantly, the exceptions tend to be specialist operations such as London Business School or promotion of process rather than content, as in the umbrella concept of a university-wide graduate school.

Much can be done to gain the benefits both of consistency and of diversity. For example, institution-wide standards may be set in regard to the format of publications and use of logos and other graphics while preserving considerable flexibility as to the content and, perhaps, the style of the message. Indeed, structure can be liberating: it is in many ways easier to create a publication around a defined skeleton than to design the whole project from a blank sheet of paper.

In these circumstances, a central marketing function offers expert advice and proposes a set of non-negotiables, otherwise allowing academic units the opportunity to express themselves.

Will there be a balance of competence? There is a danger that academic units will lack the resources to do more than dabble dangerously and incompetently in technical matters with strategic implications. It will be equally dangerous if they decide to outsource the design or writing of their material since this will divorce practice from the essential common core of agreement within the institution. An honest self-appraisal is called for. An academic unit which lacks the resource to do creative marketing work would be best advised to call upon the central service. As a result, some units may remain dependent on that service, while others run specialized marketing operations of their own. Such a difference might be appropriate to the varying needs of academic units.

Equally, there must be trust in the competence of the central office. It must decide from which parts of the institution to solicit stories and which activities to promote to the media. If academic units perceive that their own 'good stories' are being ignored while those in another unit are occupying the time and attention of the central office, resentment will set in. This situation is most likely to arise if the priorities of the central office are, for example, to gain coverage in international publications while the academic unit needs to appear regularly and positively in regional media.

We have looked here at the promotional aspects of marketing. Its more strategically central aspects such as choice and pricing of products should be of even more concern in the constant iteration of ideas within each unit and between the unit and central bodies.

Student recruitment

Student recruitment issues tend to parallel those in the field of marketing. An important point of distinction is that between undergraduate recruitment – traditionally seen as a mass, undifferentiated activity – and postgraduate recruitment – traditionally a niche level activity. Admissions are increasingly overlaid by other choices such as the number of students recruited internationally or taught overseas, or attending validated or franchised courses.

No institution can now afford to be complacent, even about UK undergraduate recruitment, the traditional 'banker' which required scarcely any effort in some institutions. The expansion of the sector, the redesignation of polytechnics as universities and the introduction of student fees and loans all suggest that the unthinkable – large numbers of unfilled places – could soon become present reality, either for whole institutions or for some subject areas. That situation would almost certainly trigger closures or, more likely, mergers of institutions or parts of institutions. Increased reliance on other students at the undergraduate level is equally unwise: will your institution be able to attract overseas students who are able to afford three years in the UK? Do you have the capability of running validated or franchised programmes both profitably and at an acceptable level of quality?

For reasons stated above, there used to be a dearth of market research about undergraduates. As research emerges, it tends to suggest that applicants are influenced by factors such as reputation of the institution, geographic preferences, availability of part-time employment and associated financial matters. The graduate employment market has grown but partly through jobs which were traditionally the preserve of non-graduates. The message is that students' choice of institution, relating to unofficial pecking orders which exist in the minds of some employers, will become increasingly important – perhaps exceeding choice of subject (other than for scientific or technical jobs) and class of degree. Research suggests that some applicants have an awareness of overall reputation, aided by *The Times Good University Guide* and by official ratings by the funding councils, though less commonly an awareness of reputation in particular subjects. Hence an issue for academic units is that they may be the unwitting beneficiary, or victim, of the institution's collective reputation. Some have attempted to rectify this situation by mounting their own schools liaison campaigns, in particular to influence school teachers who advise prospective students. This strategy is of course more readily available to departments whose subjects are well established at A level than to predominantly non-school subjects, such as philosophy or linguistics.

Nevertheless, more serious applicants will continue to research more carefully than on institution-wide reputation. There is plenty at stake for the academic unit in planning its tactics on conditional offers, dealing with applications, running open days and interviews, keeping student records and raising its profile with schools and colleges. The extent to which the unit has, or seeks, autonomy on these matters is an important aspect of its relationship with the central administration. Some units have concluded that undergraduate recruitment is too important to be left to a basic central service which in some cases still treats applicants as statistics and does not welcome personal contact with them. As units develop their own priorities, marketing, contacts, events and information systems, there is a danger that practices will become too diverse for the good of the institution. It may find itself attempting to manage intake targets which are partly constrained by funding decisions in response to market forces or, more uncomfortably, by trying to ignore market forces. Will it persist in limiting recruitment to 100 in department X, which has 1500 applicants achieving AAB at A level, while maintaining the intake of 100 in department Y from 600 applicants and an intake entering with CDD or lower? Some will point out that the A level route is now less important in their institution because of increased reliance on mature students who do not possess the qualification. Nevertheless the same issues of standards, balance and institutional quality still apply.

At undergraduate level, decisions about the location of functions as between the centre and academic units will be influenced by considerations of efficiency as well as quality. The offices must be capable of handling a large volume of work efficiently. At postgraduate level, economies of scale are not so apparent. Enquiries and applications tend to require a customized, as well as partly standard, response. There is no clearing house for applications so the institution is in the dark about the status of the enquiry or application. Most postgraduate officers believe that speed and quality of response are closely related to success in recruitment. Applicants are bound to be influenced by the attitude which is evident from the institution: did they write back within two days or two weeks? Did they bother to answer the question or merely send the prospectus? How long did they take to consider the application and respond? Departments which follow up all their offers to applicants with reminders, updates and information improve their chances of recruiting the student or, at the very least, knowing early on that he or she is going elsewhere.

This is all a matter of priority and resources. Some institutions have allowed their central postgraduate offices to become understaffed or to perform poorly in terms of customer response, despite evidence that the penalty will be loss of students and of income. Some have no substantial recruitment presence at faculty level, either. In units where postgraduate recruitment is a high priority, a dedicated office is a necessity. It can be made cost-effective by doubling as the office which services current students, hence avoiding the danger that a year-round service is set up for the sake of seasonal recruitment activities. If the unit comprises several large programmes, then it may be most cost-effective to handle recruitment at the level of the department or programme. This preserves the ability to react very quickly to enquiries and applications, whereas a faculty postgraduate office might have to lose time by referring applications, which are all in effect 'non-standard', to a selector. The disadvantage of delegation to the operational level is increased likelihood of fragmentation, inconsistency and too large variations in speed of response. Wherever located, the postgraduate office should be placing enquiries and applications on database, constantly reviewing their status and analysing its performance in recruitment year on year. This is essential because the market for every postgraduate employment programme is unique so that generalizations about trends and institutional reputation may not apply. Each has its own life cycle and should maximize the extent to which it holds its destiny in its own hands.

Studying the competition and analysing the behaviour of applicants inform the process of identifying new markets and deciding whether and how to change the product or programme. Naturally the same process should be going on for undergraduate programmes but at postgraduate level it becomes more complex and variable in its conclusions programme by programme. Volatility at postgraduate level is increased by the state of graduate employment markets and, on taught programmes, by the fact that students are on course for only a year. Successes and failures in recruitment have direct effects only for that short period whereas the recruitment effects for undergraduate or doctoral programmes last for three or more years, making the latter less immediately subject to the vagaries of the market.

Institutions have sought to reduce their vulnerability by spreading their risks, recruiting actively in several countries or seeking contracts which guarantee substantial numbers of students for several years at a time. This is a way of escaping from the demanding and often cost-ineffective cycle of recruiting individual by individual. Whether in the form of an agreement brokered by the British Council for classes of international students or a contract with a company which sends its managers on post-experience programmes, the unit may find welcome ways of spreading its risks across a wider range of activities.

Those at the centre of the institution should appreciate that the judgements to be made about provision in niche markets are so detailed and specialized that they should be left to the units themselves. While there may be overall targets to be achieved, the manner in which they are achieved is a matter for local determination. Nevertheless, there are examples of paths being blocked by central action or, even worse, senior officers signing up for programmes on behalf of academic units which are then expected to deliver something which is inappropriate as to product, place or price!

Facilities

The provision of facilities is an area which has attracted a lot of interest in debates about the relative responsibilities of central functions and academic units. Issues include charging for space, management of residences, landscaping, local catering services, reprographics, portering and cleaning, new building, minor works, furniture and maintenance.

It differs from some of the other battlegrounds in that it is a 'non-core' matter. Whereas it would be unthinkable for the institution to subcontract its academic planning or quality assurance processes, it has no necessary expertise in facilities management. Whether it should employ its own staff, professionally qualified or otherwise, or contract in the services required is a genuine question. Units are distanced from the issues by the fact that they normally have no expertise to offer, in contrast to discussions about course changes or teaching methods. As a result they tend to be treated as non-paying customers, and often rather ignorant ones. The reality is that they *are* paying customers in that some of the funds they have earned are deployed by the Buildings or Estates Office but, unless the institution has a transparent resource allocation model, the extent of the payment is not identifiable.

Practices have become highly variable across the system. In many institutions, there are now services operating on a business footing and working for academic units in which needs are identified, reported and paid for. In some places, more of the old-style public sector culture persists. Cuts in expenditure become an excuse for negligent response to problems and the absence of anything which might be described as a service, let alone a shared business-like relationship such as might be reflected in a service level agreement with academic units. The units find themselves paying for central services which operate unsatisfactorily, and often without a remedy. They often lack the budget, the knowledge, the time or the freedom to contract in external services to paint the walls, repair the chairs, replace the lightbulbs, cut the grass, collect the litter and clean the windows. These apparently minor problems, if left unattended, turn into serious issues affecting the morale of students and staff and, whether logically or not, they become symbolic of the standing of the organization.

Staffing policies can cause difficulties in that many institutions centrally recruit and manage porters, cleaners and tradespeople, then assign them to jobs in departments and buildings around the campus. This opens up the possibility that such staff are in effect permanently deployed within an academic unit and yet are not directly answerable to it; in fact, they are sometimes subject to little direct supervision from the centre either.

When services are commissioned centrally and provided locally, one of the chief gains should be that institutional expertise and wisdom is employed in order to gain the best deals for the benefit of all users, and much effort is saved by the units which need give scarcely any thought to commissioning the service. So much for theory. When the cleaning staff is halved or the photocopiers break down simultaneously, managers in the academic units suddenly have to react to problems not of their making and without the benefit of expertise or authority to solve them. Dependence on central service is rational where the scale of the activity would make it inappropriate for there to be a host of locally managed services. However, in those cases it is imperative that the institution can hold central services accountable for the quality of their performance.

New buildings and minor works – which normally mean *major* works to the lay person – raise the stakes further. In these situations, academic units are dependent on the professional expertise of architects, builders and surveyors. Such larger projects often engage the interest of the professionals concerned, with the result that the customer in the unit receives a comparatively good service. Experience suggests that, particularly when the unit itself is funding the project, a team of professionals is willing to bring alive the preferences of the department. It is they who set the pace, pushing for approval of drawings and specifications, and taking pride in the appearance of the finished product. All this is quite the reverse of some units' experience of routine maintenance functions.

In cases where units are running commercial operations, they may be able to staff their own facilities, such as a training centre or a research laboratory, in which case they may be free to set their own standards of management, though not necessarily of maintenance. In such cases, substandard services are unacceptable because they directly threaten income streams. Some managers in higher education still fail to understand how it is possible to be worse off as a result of making savings: a minor reduction in expenditure can cause a decline in service which leads to a more than proportionate loss of business. That scenario can occur even outside the commercial post-experience sector. For example, students who suffer unreasonably poor levels of support from the library and computing services advise their friends against taking up a place at that institution.

Academic units and their students are often not treated as customers in the area of facilities management. The move towards greater choice, such as in residences and in catering, is to be welcomed because it helps the student to pay for what he or she wants and can afford. Too many institutions have barely begun the journey to customer orientation and may get there only if the academic units demand better value for money. An era of greater flexibility could arise in that shrinking central budgets can be supplemented by discretionary spending by academic units to make decent standards attainable once again.

Quality

Relative responsibilities for quality, and the management of quality, are changing. In pre-audit days, quality management had a place at institutional level, albeit in most HEIs considerable autonomy was allowed to faculties and departments provided that their procedures were consistent and justifiable. The culture was based on trust. In practice, the status of the individual teacher was considered sufficient to guarantee that aims and objectives were appropriate, that methods of teaching and assessment were consistent with those aims and objectives and that the course was well-managed, reviewed and improved. In the traditional model, the initial course proposal – not always produced in standard format – supported by a bibliography often provided the only opportunity for colleagues and the rest of the institution to comment upon the course. Thereafter, some sampling of students' work by an external examiner might be the only occasion for review. Unless serious problems broke out in a public manner, the teacher was sovereign, lord or lady of his or her own private garden.

Vestiges of that time still remain and are regarded with disturbingly fond nostalgia by many academics. No doubt in institutions blessed with able, committed teachers and resourceful students, such lightness of touch was acceptable and often beneficial. In these same institutions were also examples of misdirected or ineffective teaching, poor attention to students' progress and a cavalier attitude to deadlines and marking. HEIs now bemoan the lack of trust implicitly shown by the very existence of bodies such as the Quality Assurance Agency. However, it is their own reluctance to introduce a more systematic approach to quality of teaching and its management which has opened the door to the auditors.

This is not to fall into the trap of confusing management of quality with quality itself. Sceptical academics have taken delight in the evident difficulty of defining the concept of quality. That may have won some debating points, but it has not swayed the argument. Those in favour of audit have often given the impression that the procedures for the management of quality are more important in their minds than the quality of provision itself. As a result, HEIs have learned to become much more vigilant and to cover their backs by documenting more decisions and holding more reviews than they used to. Being professional thinkers and writers, academics have become adept at writing convincing self-assessments, statements of aims and objectives and annual reports. Unfortunately, the feeling of game-playing and jumping through hoops helps to bring about a widening gap in academics' minds between the reality in the classroom and how it is described on paper. Uncomfortable experience has now led some academics to produce more bland reports: they fear that by cataloguing problems and suggesting remedies, they will expose themselves to 'continuation audit' at every level from their own faculty upwards.

It is not understood by the public that an institution might have high standards in the regulation of its procedures while its students produce low standards of work and its teachers lack an intellectual edge. Like a financial audit which examines the propriety and application of procedures but tells you nothing about business performance except (arguably) the measure of profitability, so the academic audit compares policies with practices without getting to the heart of what is taught and the quality of the students and their performance.

It is at the level of the institution that the buck must stop, not in departments, faculties or schools – they do not award degrees.

There is nothing wrong with delegation of authority. But it needs effective oversight to ensure that delegation does not become abnegation.

> (Peter Williams, Director of Institutional Review,
> Quality Assurance Agency for Higher Education,
> Letter to *The Times Higher*, 9 January 1998)

Sharing of responsibilities within the institution may need formal recognition or acknowledgement. The need for a formal, legal agreement between collaborating institutions has been generally accepted (although by no means universally practised). But there may also be a need for a 'compact' between the centre and the faculties since otherwise people can just shuffle off their responsibilities.

> (Roger Brown, formerly Chief Executive,
> Higher Education Quality Council,
> *The Times Higher*, 19 December 1997)

Geoffrey Alderman, Pro-Vice-Chancellor (quality and audit) at Middlesex University, said: 'The QAA is obsessed with corporate responsibility for standards but the sector is moving in the opposite direction, delegating more to faculties and departments' (quoted in *The Times Higher*, 30 July 1999).

The buzz-word of the Nineties in higher education is 'quality'. We have quality research, quality teaching, quality audits, quality students in quality institutions; and we ensure it is maintained by quality assurance mechanisms that are monitored by quality control groups. We even have a quality assurance agency, to help us sleep more easily in our beds, untroubled by nightmares about unimproved quality.

With all this going on, it seems almost churlish to ask why so many of us are sceptical. Obviously, the bottom line is that students are entitled to a good education, academics are entitled to good working conditions and the taxpayer is entitled to value for money from universities. Also having some form of peer review of teaching, research output and infrastructure is a good thing. But in pursuit of this chimera, we are in danger of creating a monstrous, Kafka-esque system in which teams of assessors trundle in perpetuity round the country's universities inspecting quality. Or rather, inspecting what they tell us quality ought to be. Because there are all sorts of definitions of quality. For a start, universities should prioritize teaching and learning, we are told. No point in saying that this is what universities have been doing for a thousand years. These days, you have to fill in the forms that prove you have demonstrable quality learning outputs.

What is happening in higher education is a dumbing down of the whole system, under the pretext of improving quality for all. The myth is being circulated that all British universities are, and should be, indentical in terms of quality. This is a good selling-point for ministers who want to persuade overseas students to part with their cash and come to Britain. But it is patently untrue. There are bad universities, good universities and excellent universities and no amount of juggling of statistics is going to make those differences go away. The reality is that in all universities countless hours are spent preparing paperwork to demonstrate the quality of teaching or of research. Weak universities want to show that they are as good as Cambridge, or Warwick, and so pour their efforts into making sure they score where the paperwork is concerned. Because what counts in all this quality control business is knowing how to get the documentation right. You can prove that geese are swans, if you learn the jargon effectively.

So the people who have been promoted because they were reckoned to be the best teachers or researchers can no longer do either because they are too busy preparing the documentation. Ensuring quality is ensuring jobs (a lot better paid than academics' jobs, too) for people who never managed to win many accolades for their own research or teaching and, increasingly, for people who have never taught or researched anything in their lives. There is a whole new cadre of university bureaucrats living comfortably off the quality industry.

All this is presented as being in the interests of students. But I believe students get a raw deal. For a start, their tutors are having to put most of their energy into dealing with the bureaucracy.

Well over 70 per cent of my time goes on paperwork these days. In many institutions, one way round this is to employ postgraduates to do most of the teaching, leaving senior academics time to fill in more quality control forms. Students may go to a university to work in a department made famous by dedicated scholars and teachers, and rarely meet them. The sheer amount of work that students are expected to do has dropped radically over the past decade. Amid all the talk of maintaining quality despite rising numbers, it is easy to forget how the operation has been managed. One way has been a reduction in student workload. Let's take a hypothetical example: if a group of 15 students writes six essays a year, that is a total of 90 essays for the tutor to mark. Increase that group to 30, put them in a larger lecture room, and they can still have the same contact hours. The university can say, with honesty, that the standards of teaching remain the same. But there is no way that the same tutor can be expected to mark 180 essays in the same amount of time. What happens? The essay requirements are cut. Thirty students writing four essays a year still gives the tutor an increased workload, but the impact on the students is a reduction in hours of work.

I am reminded every day of Hans Andersen's emperor, who was conned into believing that he had the finest robes in creation until he was exposed as naked by a small child. It is time the students themselves blew the whistle on all this quality-speak before it damages higher education beyond repair.

Let there be peer reviews by all means, and let's insist that universities set up the sort of rigorous self-monitoring systems that we have in place at Warwick. But let's call a halt to the procession of naked fat cats funding their timeshares in Tenerife on quality assurance, so that we can get back to doing what universities are supposed to do – i.e. educating the next generation.

(Susan Bassnett, Pro-Vice-Chancellor,
University of Warwick, *The Independent*,
12 February 1998)

Academic standards can never be guaranteed primarily through written procedures. Such procedures can help, but are ancillary to the scholastic professionalism of teachers and students. The key to the maintenance of academic standards is staff development. Academic audit had many strengths, but two of its major weaknesses were its inability to appreciate the pivotal importance of non-documented scholarly dialogue and its obsession with formal paperwork. This was why Oxford and Cambridge received such negative audit reports.

The recent report presented by the History at the Universities Defence Group to the QAA reaches the same broad conclusions. 'Only the professional historian is equipped to determine what constitutes mastery of the subject of history', with the inevitable consequence that only professional historians can legitimately judge the assurance of standards of history courses. Continuation audit appears unequal to the task of addressing these issues, preferring to concentrate on the much easier target of 'corporate responsibility' for standards, as evidenced in formal procedures. Such an approach would be laughable were it not so irresponsible and potentially so damaging.

(Geoffey Alderman, Pro-Vice-Chancellor,
Middlesex University, *The Times Higher*,
26 December 1997)

Assessment, as distinct from audit, of quality does venture to examine standards. However, the extent to which assessment of quality is relative to mission is a source of difficulty. For example, an institution which set itself restricted, modest goals and achieved them consistently would be rated as qualitatively superior to one which was able to achieve only 75 per cent of the challenging goals it had set itself. Which would be the better place to work or study? To avoid this problem, the assessment of quality would have to rate teachers and students through some kind of objective standard. Although credit could be given for high levels of value added, a ranked list would tend to correspond closely to the institutions which were best resourced and attracted the students with the best entry qualifications. The process would tend to reinforce the status quo.

The movement away from the autonomy of the individual teacher has placed the onus on the institution to demonstrate the effectiveness of its quality procedures. In an area in which consistency is all important, the focus of attention is directed towards the centre of the institution. Practice in academic units and by individuals is placed within an institutional framework so that policy on matters such as the permitted proportions of coursework assessment, the duration and intensity of modules, schemes for allocating marks, standards regarding the timing of the submission and return of assessed work, should be worked out in a central forum in which all academic units are represented. Each institution decides for itself the degree to which such policies should be prescribed and the relative importance of each policy.

The imposition of a single policy, even within a diverse institution, need not prove stifling provided that some degree of latitude is permissible and some matters are left to local determination.

Whatever control and choice is located at the level of the academic unit, it is imperative that the unit manages those areas of activity with the utmost attention to detail. It is not acceptable to pass on problems to the central administration. Equally the onus is on the central administration to ensure that its processes and systems are of comparable quality with those in the academic units. If comparability of standards is not maintained, there will be inevitable demands to remove and replace the poor-performing services with the result that the institution finds itself under pressure to move towards, or away from, greater devolution of responsibilities without having made a policy decision on the matter.

When it comes to following good practice, a choice may have to made between locating the guardians of quality in the central administration or in academic units. A central office may be necessary to run the boundary between the academic units and external bodies, interpreting one to the other. That office is not likely to be in a good position to affect detailed, day-to-day actions which determine the extent to which quality is maintained and managed. It may become a surrogate for external bodies, nagging the operational units into conformity. There is some value in the existence somewhere of such a watchdog but it is doubtful whether the value added is sufficient to justify much of the cost of a central office.

Perhaps the greatest value which a central office can impart is in the area of dissemination of good practice. Auditors find pockets of good practice, some of which is innovative, but most institutions are not adept at mutual learning. Even within an academic unit, communications are often insufficient to enable others to adopt and adapt practices which have been shown to work well. Cross-learning between faculties is even less common. The 'not-invented-here' syndrome is at least as deeply entrenched in academia as it is in large companies so, at some level, someone should be responsible for spotting good ideas and bringing them into a forum comprising receptive people. The size, complexity and diversity of the institution may indicate whether such an informing, facilitating role is best located within each substantial academic unit or at the centre.

The greatest danger in those institutions committed to conforming to the requirements of audit and assessment is that actual quality will be obscured by the management of quality. Some external examiners experience institutions in which systems and procedures seem extremely well regulated and yet the quality of the work produced by the students is very poor. Uninspired students and uninspiring lecturers are capable of going through the motions of higher education and of satisfying many of the criteria which are likely to appear on a quality agenda. It would certainly be self-defeating if academic leaders were to turn away from implementing bold, innovative and experimental ideas. If the experience is to be challenging, then not every element will necessarily be predictable and defined.

7

BUILDING A SUPPORT TEAM

Academics and administrators: comparative advantages

What priorities should govern the creation of support services within the unit? Clearly the answer will be contingent upon the nature of activities (Who are the clients? How technical is the subject matter?) and their scale and complexity.

Some guidelines may be applicable throughout the system. An academic performing a leadership role, such as dean, chair of faculty board or warden of residences, is immediately exposed to incoming messages, requests for decisions, attendance at meetings and demands for information. It is virtually impossible to cope in these circumstances if one is undertaking the organizational role part-time since one remains committed to teaching, other projects and research which require absence from the office. The availability of a personal assistant, even if only part-time, is necessary to manage the communications and diary. Finding a basic level of support is not a matter of self-aggrandizement or perfectionism; it is a necessity, if only because the lack of it will land the post-holder in embarrassing situations resulting from failed communications and broken deadlines. There are sufficient reasons to lose face and for others to deem you to be incompetent without bringing about such a situation through simple lack of support! Hence bargaining for it should be a part of anyone's acceptance of a significant organizational role.

Having secured one's own office, at least for the foreseen demands which will be placed upon it, you will need to plan for senior roles through which your unit will be managed and taken forward. There are a range of choices, conditioned of course by what is already in existence. For example, you may find your unit already populated by departments with adequate support structures of their own, leaving you to plan for add-on activities or for restructuring in the medium to long term. At the other end of the scale, you may be in a small start-up situation which may be expected to grow rapidly.

The senior roles you may require are likely to include the management of teaching programmes, of research projects, of commercial relationships, of collaborative relationships with other providers, of budgets and finance, of building projects, and of personnel. These roles will vary greatly in the amounts of time they demand and in the skills needed to fulfil them. The person who visits companies to 'sell' your unit and to sign up managers to join your post-experience programme is not likely to be the same person who coordinates the plans and specifications of the extension to your building.

Unless the enterprise is very small, you will be wise to create a small management team but it alone is not likely to carry out all the activities that are required. You need to be clear about what you can expect from others. In the gentlemanly atmosphere which still persists in some corners of academia, specific outcomes and timetables are sometimes left unstated. This is a big mistake! Many are the times that I have seen deans or directors express frustration or delight at the unexpected actions of academic staff. To avoid the sense of personal and organizational disappointment, the leader can encourage active participation of others by inviting them to set out their own preferred remit. If it accords with the unit's needs and with the leader's intentions, so much the better; if not, it can be negotiated. The discussion should include broad agreement about the nature of acceptable outcomes, amounts of time required and target dates.

Some tasks have to be undertaken, or at least led, by senior academics. For example, advising members of faculty about subjects to research and how best to prepare articles for publication, targeting suitable journals, is a job for a head of department or an associate dean for research.

There are many other tasks – such as acting as admissions tutor (undergraduate and postgraduate), examinations secretary, student adviser, departmental careers adviser, placements manager, director of facilities (such as laboratories or equipment), safety officer, monitor of budgets, manager of support staff such as technicians and secretaries, representatives of the unit on committees, writer of course descriptions, annual reports and prospectus entries, planner of timetables – and a host of other duties most of which are particular to the needs of a department. These tasks have traditionally been carried out by the academic staff, usually with some allowance of time.

Heads of department have faced the unpleasant task of parcelling out such duties among staff who are unenthusiastic about them and in some cases incompetent to carry them out. There have been instances of deliberately acquired incompetence, designed to ensure that such work never comes one's way again. The increased burden associated with such administration is a major source of complaint from heads of department and others. Heads are the most likely to complain about the increased prominence of quality assurance because they have to shoulder an added burden as a direct result. Time and energy for research, even for teaching, is eroded with negative consequences for morale and productivity. Neither do the sums make sense. Should people paid as a professor or senior lecturer spend significant amounts of time on relatively mundane administrative duties for which they normally have no aptitude or training? Sometimes the work is not even done well – with disastrous consequences. A negligent, ill-organized postgraduate admissions tutor can wreak havoc on the academic and financial health of a department by responding as if there were a guaranteed queue of eager applicants beating down the door for admission. And yet some heads of department frequently reassign the job in response to the current holder's desire to be rid of it, and let it fall, like a punishment, on another colleague.

It would be an exaggeration to claim that, on the traditional model, academic staff undertake administrative tasks unaided. They often make full use of secretaries – someone like the versatile paragon caricatured as Maureen in Laurie Taylor's column in *The Times Higher*. Even this apparently rational behaviour can cause problems. For example, as the overwhelmed academic finds ways of sharing, delegating or dumping work on the departmental secretary, so that person's job expands and becomes more responsible. If the secretary swims rather than sinks, a justifiable case for a regrading arises, often accompanied by a bid for an additional junior secretary to absorb the less demanding work in the office. It is good to see career progression in action, but one effect will have been to add £15,000 (say £3,000 for the regrading and £12,000 for the new post) to the current budget. Apart from that, because the whole thing was probably unplanned, the departmental secretary will have been struggling to acquire new skills such as learning to use a financial reporting system, supervising other staff, advising students and creating record systems. The post-holder may possibly have been promoted beyond a natural comfort zone and begun to operate somewhat below the level of competence desired by the organization. Better results might have been achieved by establishing a plan for the reassignment of duties from the head of department to an officer capable of

Table 7.1 Academic and administrative roles for a programme

Academic director (part-time: 10–20%)	*Administrative manager (full-time)*
Strategy and development of programme.	Marketing of programme.
Advice to teaching staff on nature of inputs and learning.	Organization of timetable, classes and tutorials.
Contact with students for admissions interviews and dealing with exceptional problems.	Management of assessment processes.
	Everyday management of student affairs.
Overall responsibility for quality assurance and management of exceptional issues.	Management of quality control processes, drawing attention to exceptional issues.
Representation of programme to prospective clients and external examiner.	Routine contact with clients and external examiner.
	Working with or supervision of programme secretary.

operating at a relatively senior administrative level with an appreciation of policy implications.

The extent to which professional administrative staff should be used is a major decision. There are some disadvantages: the unit may be perceived as having hired a bureaucracy of people who make no direct contribution to teaching and research and, the greater their influence, the more members of faculty will become distanced from student affairs. In some schools the faculty inhabit the top floors of the building, working like monks in cells, occasionally going downstairs to take a class.

However, on the positive side, the use of administrative staff working closely with academics offers the opportunity for academics to be involved without being overwhelmed. In the current financial climate, facing the distraction of a heavy administrative load is not a rational situation for an academic whose knowledge is required to deliver teaching programmes and who faces pressure to publish at least one article a year in the best possible journals. For those who are exempted from either the teaching role or from the research role, expectations are correspondingly doubled in that person's remaining specialism. However, it is quite feasible for academic staff to hold a demanding role such as director of a teaching programme without damaging mainstream priorities, provided that an administrator/manager can take on its day-to-day running. A division of duties might look like Table 7.1 for a major part-time post-experience teaching programme.

Although Table 7.1 suggests a separation of duties, in fact the major areas of responsibility are shared. The essence of successful programme management is teamwork and good communications.

Location of work: at the centre or in the unit?

If you decided that the unit needs professional administrative support in order that the academic director, senior management team and directors of programmes may function efficiently, the next questions are: what kind of administrator do you seek, and from where?

There will be a need to cover 'faculty office' functions whatever the size of the operation while the extent of support required for teaching programmes, research projects or for the management of finance, quality, marketing, personnel and facilities matters is variable according to the strategy of the unit. The faculty office normally coordinates the activities of the constituent academic departments and sections, presents cases and responds on behalf of the collectivity, organizes committees and working parties which set policy, plans and approves academic proposals and conveys recommendations to central institutional bodies, and forms a central point for student registration data, records and assessment procedures.

That profile of work is mainstream higher education administration since the functions essentially correspond to those in the central administration. Indeed they could all be carried out in full within the centre or alternatively almost wholly within the faculty office which shares with the centre databases and reports in electronic or paper form. Some institutions opt for a compromise or, more uneasily, allow the balance of control and responsibility to vacillate between the centre and the unit. In most cases, the preferred operating level is the unit, provided that the unit is resourced to do the work. If it is not, then a centre which nevertheless devolves responsibility would appear to be negligent. The reason to prefer the maximum amount of competent local control is that those closest to the action are most likely to know the facts. Anything which reduces the costs of running a central bureaucracy remote from academic operations is also to be welcomed. A business school in one university found advantages in local control (see Box 7.1).

Recognizing the core nature of most faculty office functions, some institutions have seconded members of the central administration to a faculty, sometimes by moving them physically. There are clear advantages in this approach: the registrar maintains control in that a central appointee continues to report to him or her and indeed the faculty administrator acts as an extra pair of eyes and ears, a

---

Box 7.1 Should student records be managed centrally or in academic units?

To an outsider making an enquiry about a student who studied at a university, a centrally held records department is an advantage. If records are held in individual schools, the enquirer has to have details of what the student studied to know where to begin. However, central record-keeping can create difficulties for the units.

In one case, where a school controlled the entering and updating both of the academic and personal records of its students, support staff in the school accepted responsibility for ensuring that the records were accurate and took pride in their ability to do a good job. When the data entry moved to a central unit, those entering the data did not know whether the information they were entering was accurate because they did not know the courses they were dealing with, nor the students. Where it would be obvious to school staff that a student on a particular programme could not be studying a particular module, it was not obvious to the central unit entering the data. Mistakes were not spotted, inaccurate data were supplied and no one accepted responsibility – the central unit said the schools supplied the wrong information and the schools said it was an error in data entry by the central unit.

By all means have a central unit that holds student records, but ensure that there is ownership of the data by giving those that collect the data the responsibility of entering it into the system.

---

conduit for information flowing both ways; the academic head of unit becomes better networked, gaining direct access to an administrator who can report back on current developments and rumours; and the administrator gains valuable, virtually hands-on experience of an academic unit while to some extent escaping the more uniform world of central administration. Some institutions rotate staff in such positions so as to diversify experience and guard against staleness or conflict. There are risks inherent in the arrangement. The administrator who reports to the registrar, but works for the head of unit day-to-day, is quite likely to have to deal with different, possibly conflicting, demands. While the 'two bosses' syndrome is not as difficult as some people claim, hard choices about what to tell whom do arise. Career benefits are limited, particularly if the academic unit is not a large player nationally. One may develop one's career so far but no further by working in some fields, although schools of business, engineering, medicine or dentistry offer distinctive and attractive career prospects. Some other subjects form a large unit in a few institutions, while not figuring in many others. Another potential danger for the faculty administrator is that 'out of sight, out of mind', he or she may find the secondment lasting longer than desired and a lack of career-enhancing routes back to the centre. A prolonged absence from the centre may inhibit the administrator's ability to stay well informed and consequently to add maximum value to his or her role in the unit.

Assignment to a faculty without a physical posting is a somewhat half-hearted version of specialized administration. Unless the administrator works to free up considerable amounts of time to talk to academic colleagues, the arrangement can be too arm's length to be much more effective than the traditional fully centralized model. Moving to an office in a faculty and working from there, preferably full-time, is undoubtedly a liberating experience as it becomes clear that communications between academics and administrators are much more effective.

Drafts can be agreed and briefings circulated within minutes and, more important, the symbolism of locating an administrator at the centre of an academic operation is an eloquent statement about the perceived importance of the unit.

A physical move can be seen as raising the stakes for an administrator, particularly if there is no early prospect of an end to the secondment. On the one hand, the opportunity to work closely with a set of academic staff may boost the administrator's morale and feeling of self-worth as successful joint working can produce an atmosphere which wholly replaces the seemingly inevitable 'them' and 'us' feeling between an academic unit and a central administration. On the other hand, if the work or relationships prove unsatisfactory, the administrator could have a sense of being trapped in an uncongenial environment from which there is no ready escape, while the academics may feel lumbered with an underperforming administrator through whom they are forced to operate.

Having negotiated an appropriate level of local, or earmarked central, support, and decided how it wishes to employ its academic workforce in relation to organizational duties, the academic unit has to assess its needs against services available. Thus far, we have considered administrative support of the basic kind required to coordinate policy and communications internally and to run activities based within the unit. What about the services which the unit may find supplied from the centre? These include:

- finance
- buildings, maintenance and cleaning
- personnel
- marketing, including public relations
- student recruitment
- student advice and counselling
- quality assurance
- careers advice
- support for research
- printing and photography
- technology for teaching
- library and IT services.

These functions are worth studying because it will probably be the case that up to 40 per cent of the unit's income is being diverted to cover the cost of such central services. The way in which funds are calculated should be transparent. Traditionally, the units would pay an undifferentiated tax so that, for example, the English Department would lose, say, 5 per cent of its income to cover Buildings and Estates functions even though only 1 per cent of the Buildings and Estates budget was spent on the English Department. Injustices of this kind have led to the introduction of more carefully costed systems which have encouraged the providing services to become more customer oriented. In some cases service level agreements have been created to clarify the respective expectations of the internal customer (the academic unit) and of the supplier (the central service). Implicit or explicit in this is the possibility that a dissatisfied internal customer could take the business elsewhere, for example by contracting with an external company to clean or redecorate the building. There are often brakes on such action because the central service is committed to staffing and other costs which cannot be run down in the short term. Nevertheless, the injection of commercial awareness is a healthy antidote to the monopoly supplier and opaque budget situation which can sometimes prevail.

Another source of pressure in recent years has been a relentless bearing down on central administrative costs. When referred to as 'overheads', activities are made to sound dispensable. In reality, reducing overheads normally means cutting staff and worsening the services supplied. However, in some cases there was previously a combination of sufficient or generous staffing and poor management, so that a fresh approach to management has sometimes maintained quality of service despite cuts in resources. Such outcomes can usually be achieved only once, so that further cuts do almost inevitably damage services.

Table 7.2 Departments' demand for central services

Central service	English Department	Physics Department	Business School
Finance	Low	High	Average
Buildings, maintenance, cleaning	Low	High	Average–high
Personnel	Low	High	Average
Marketing, including public relations	Low–average	High	High
Student recruitment	Low	High	Low
Student advice and counselling	Average	Average	Average
Quality assurance	Average	Average	Average
Careers advice	High (or should be)	Average	Low–average
Support for research	Low	High	Low–average
Printing and photography	Average	Average–high	High
Technology for teaching	Low–average	Average–high	Average–high
Library	Average	Average	Low–average
IT	Low	High	Average

Those kinds of issues might affect academic units on a roughly equal basis. Others do not, because of academic units' differential needs. For example, consider three departments' levels of demand for the central services listed above, as shown in Table 7.2.

This crude analysis shows why it is more expensive to run a Physics Department than an English Department – a fact recognized by differential levels of funding and fees. Zoom-in to get a more informative view, for example by taking four of the line items in detail (Table 7.3).

Where a department places an above-average demand on a central service, questions arise: is the central service resourced to respond, or can it not do so without unfairly disadvantaging departments which have an average or below-average demand for the service? Can a sufficient level of quality be delivered? Is there a fair method of apportioning costs so that heavy users are seen to pay more than light users? A department may find that its demand exceeds the resources available from the centre, or that the level of quality provided is below an acceptable level, or that it is charged excessively for the service it receives. It may lobby the central service for a

Table 7.3 Explanation of variable demand for central services

	English Department	Physics Department	Business School
Personnel	Low turnover of staff, few non-academic appointments.	Large number of non-academic and research staff on fixed-term contracts.	Above-average turnover of academic staff and expansion.
Marketing, including public relations	85 per cent of students are UK undergraduates recruited through the prospectus. Postgraduate and undergradmate places are filled through the prospectus and from direct approaches. Demand is buoyant at all levels.	Insufficient applications are received. Energy and imagination in marketing the department are required in order to attract enough good quality students.	Demand for taught courses buoyant but always a competitive threat from other schools at MBA level. High quality marketing needed to maintain profile and to attract scarce research students.
Student recruitment	The main demand is processing a high volume of applications. No additional effort is required.	Department seeks assistance from the centre in promoting its programmes.	As for English Department.
Careers advice	Students experience problems in finding satisfactory employment. They should be pressing Careers to put additional effort into identifying job opportunities.	Students mostly readily employable, but require basic guidance.	Students mostly readily employable and some have work experience. Many take the initiative in identifying jobs.

better deal or, if that is not forthcoming, it may decide to identify its own additional or alternative service, either by outsourcing (engaging an external contractor) or by buying in (setting up its own staff position). This assumes that the institution allows it to do so: it is possible that, having invested in setting up a central service, it cannot afford departments to claim exemption from their share of running costs. Therefore it is more likely that a department will contemplate an additional, rather than a replacement, service.

To use the examples given above, it is possible that the functions of personnel and recruitment-related marketing are so important to the Physics Department that it should set aside funds to employ its own staff to work with, but significantly beyond, the central services in those areas. Doing so may be the only way to achieve the level of service required for the smooth operation – possibly even the survival – of the department. Similarly, the business school may find that, in order to compete with the specialized marketing functions of its rivals, it must identify resources (in-house or contracted from an agency) to promote itself through the media. The central services would be unlikely to have sufficient or relevant experience to meet that need on behalf of the business school.

The financial implications of acting in these ways can prove uncomfortable all round. The department feels that it is paying twice in that it is likely still to be taxed to cover the cost of central services which it deems to be inadequate! Future collaboration is not eased by a sense of rejection which central officers may feel, even if the whole process has been quite amicable and based on a rational analysis of 'horses for courses'.

When a unit decides to make appointments of its own, there are several points to be borne in mind. Before outsourcing anything, think particularly carefully. If the lack of a service is seen as important, there is a tendency among academic staff to dismiss internal solutions as ineffective and, as specialized experts themselves, to prefer the services of a specialist. The use of consultants or agents in matters such as public relations, IT support and recruitment of international students are examples of services which are sometimes outsourced.

Be sceptical of the professional sales pitch which will be aimed at a group of academic staff who are not necessarily worldly wise. Be prepared to pay high prices: the agent is in business to make a profit whereas your own employees need receive only a salary. Bear in mind that those who make the presentation to pitch for your business may not be the same people who will actually work on your behalf: the senior partner who sounds so knowledgeable about your needs may delegate the actual tasks to less experienced, less able people. Be under no illusions: you are not solving a problem by paying others to take the burden from your shoulders. For the arrangement to achieve anything for you, you will still have to commit the time of your own senior people to ensure that your agents are provided with material, given guidance and of course monitored.

You have to assess the value of the expertise you are buying. Is it really something beyond your own resources? Can you achieve the desired outcomes through your own direct efforts? Be satisfied also that you are willing for your reputation to be used and developed by an agency. Will it maintain your standing or could it cause you damage?

These sceptical questions may encourage the thought that if the activity is of basic importance to your operation, you should manage it yourself. Whether the function is specialized or general, whether supplementing a central service or creating something particular to your unit, you may be on the verge of building a team without knowing it. Unless you have a clear long-range plan, you may not know how large a support team you will wish to create. HEIs have more than their share of self-centred individuals whose preferences *may* be aligned with the needs of the organization. It is important to maintain balance by seeking out team-oriented people who are comfortable working with others at different levels and sharing the trials and joys of organizational life. It is worth giving early thought to the values you wish to promote since it is feasible to inculcate such values within a small, coherent core of people but much more difficult once the operation has expanded and diversified. If you can set what you regard as the appropriate tone in a small centre, there is a chance that later formed units will adopt the same values.

Some considerations affecting staff recruitment to the unit

What skills do you require?

Does your new person really need to be bilingual? Does she or he need a degree in the appropriate subject? Are eight years of experience essential? Is prior knowledge of the institution's financial or admissions systems necessary or can you allow a newcomer to learn them? All too often units prematurely close down their options and deny themselves a look at promising applicants by erecting artificial barriers. Damage can be done by parading 'essential' characteristics which turn out to be unnecessary. The person who looks forward to working with you in order to improve her second or third language may become disaffected if the job scarcely offers her the chance to do so.

HEIs have a tendency to be impressed by qualifications, particularly their own! Sometimes an overqualified applicant sets a problem.

Naturally, you would be foolish to pass over someone who has abilities which could eventually be developed beyond the boundaries of the job. However, will the unemployed graduate sit happily with the somewhat routine requirements of your grade two clerical position? At the very least, the selectors have a range of concerns to satisfy before offering an appointment to an overqualified person.

Some qualifications may be indispensable. If you are hiring a secretary who may have to draft and send letters to customers or students, you will look for reasonable standards of English beyond the level reached by the spell-check. Presumably there should be a good reason why a candidate has not obtained at least grade C at GCSE English Language. Maybe you need to set a higher standard than that.

Supplementary tests are an excellent idea, although they are still not the norm in some parts of the higher education system. On the day of interview candidates can be given a set of tests relevant to the job but they should be warned in advance. Tests have to be scrupulously fair to all who take them and should be thought out and piloted in advance. Rarely do the results prove decisive but, when combined with informal meetings and a formal interview, they often provide supporting evidence which gives greater confidence to the decision. Alternatively, they can sow the seeds of doubt and prevent a panel from rushing into a hasty decision. The extra time spent on selection is tiny in comparison with the average period of employment and is strongly recommended. Above all, the use of tests gives two messages to the candidates: first, that the job and, by implication, the post-holder, is considered important; second, that the unit sets high professional standards.

Interpersonal skills

In non-technical jobs, interpersonal skills (a suitably vague but imposing sounding term) are paramount. They may be taken to encompass qualities such as demonstrable commitment to customer relations, capacity for leadership and teamwork, willingness to volunteer, and judgement as to when to be assertive, tactful, persuasive or encouraging. Employees who possess such skills in large measure are a major asset. It is even arguable that they are 'primary' in that, if they exist and can be allied with the traditional virtues of intelligence, enthusiasm and thoroughness, then they outweigh technical skills which can all be acquired. The organization's need for people skilled in finance, general administration, report-writing or marketing may not be best met by hiring on the basis of associated qualifications.

Box 7.2 Alternative models for deployment of staff

Model A	*Staffing (all full-time)*
Programme 1 (large-scale)	Manager C, secretaries D and E
Programme 2 (medium-scale)	Manager F, secretary G
Programme 3 (small-scale)	Secretary H

Model B	*Staffing*
Programme 1 (large-scale)	Manager C, secretaries D and E
Programme 2 (medium-scale)	Manager F (75 per cent), secretary G
Programme 3 (small-scale)	Manager F (25 per cent), secretary H (50 per cent)

There are advantages in recruiting those with appropriate interpersonal skills, allied with basic educational qualifications and technical knowledge, and then developing their more advanced technical skills.

Staff management at work

Teamworking enables the unit to develop newcomers safely in that their inexperience need not be exposed and their confidence undermined by mistakes. The unit can feel more confident of outcomes, knowing that staff can cover for one another and specialize within the context of a shared operation. The disadvantage is that operations can appear to be overstaffed, even if the contributors have other roles. It can be difficult to know who is responsible and some managers are more comfortable with the notion of a single dedicated person managing a project. However, one is then vulnerable to chance factors such as illness, departure and variability of performance.

Specialization also makes rotation of jobs more difficult to implement, causing staff to stick in a rut and perhaps to adopt a parochial view, assuming their activity to be of primary importance and disregarding all else. Using full-time people to contribute part-time to various projects has advantages over the exclusive use of dedicated individuals. Box 7.2 shows two alternative models.

Model B is cheaper, saving half of a secretary. It also provides significantly more flexibility and opportunities for staff to deputize and respond knowledgeably to crises and fluctuations in workload. New activities, such as Programme 3, can be supported through part-time staffing without having to identify dedicated resources. This factor can become important if the activity should fail or otherwise have a short life, in which case there is a danger of having to redeploy redundant staff. More important still, the deployment of managers in different programmes opens the way to good practice being spread from one area to another. Model B is likely to be closer to the ideal of the 'learning organization' than Model A, although even Model A is superior to an alternative which could feature even more specialization and separation.

When looked at on a small scale such as this, the differences between Model A and Model B seem minor. However, as the extent of activities grows, and the staffing doubles or trebles, choices and potential savings become much more significant.

8

REPRESENTING THE UNIT

Who represents the unit?

It is now a commonplace that all organizations are represented as much by their front office staff as by their senior executives. The external person – whether student, client, customer, assessor, interviewee, visitor, debtor or creditor – has an initial encounter with a gatekeeper whose actions can have an important influence on that person's attitude to the organization. Even those who know that matters of substance are not settled by the porter or the receptionist find themselves affected by the treatment they receive in person or by telephone. Therefore the time and effort spent in the selection, training and briefing of front-line staff is likely to prove worthwhile. If that process is handled effectively, the staff concerned will become capable of making a substantial contribution to the goals of the organization, based upon the understanding of the issues they have acquired. For a large school, the support staff may include a receptionist, porters, secretaries, cleaners, caterers and maintenance people. For a small unit, it may comprise a part-time departmental secretary. At any point on the spectrum, the same principles apply. This philosophy of interface with the outside underlies the marketing-based approach to company organization and the standards of the Investors in People initiative which are proving as applicable in education as they are in industry.

Who represents the unit when *you* go out to *them*? How do you handle prospective clients, donors or assessors? Do those skills differ from those you require in order to deal with another faculty, the registry or a meeting of Senate?

Representing the unit externally ■

It is commonly assumed that in units with a significant professional orientation and where courses have direct vocational relevance, there is a corresponding external professional community or body with which the unit should communicate. In some subjects, it may not be clear which of several bodies should be contacted and the school may find itself in deep political waters. The importance of the external professional interface is obvious in subjects such as medicine, dentistry, engineering, law, business and accountancy, and teacher education. Other subjects, too, identify professional bodies and companies which can contribute ideas to the process of higher education and provide employment for graduates. These include psychology and the sciences. All departments have an interest in maintaining contact with their alumni, whether or not they regard them as prospective sources of funds.

Managing relationships with external constituents is normally considered to be a responsibility of the head of school, the dean or director. The leader is freed of most teaching, perhaps also of research, responsibilities in order to study and direct energy towards the set of external concerns which affect the school. In a small humanities department, external effort may, for instance, centre upon the need to recruit annually ten to fifteen international students in order to maintain income, quality of teaching and a lively programme of research. In a large professional school, there may be a similar objective, but magnified thirty-fold, along with the need to run a post-experience programme for serving professionals, a case to be made for the accreditation of teaching programmes, high-quality financial management to support a campaign to raise funds for new facilities or staffing and a dedicated media relations operation to enhance the public standing of the school.

It is likely that, in the latter case, the dean or director would need to create a professional support team with specialists in areas such as international links and recruitment, post-experience education, finance, fund-raising and public relations. Naturally such specialists add significantly to the overhead costs, and they will be justifiable according to the scale of current and prospective operations. The dean would expect to spend up to 70 per cent of each very full week with external constituents, for example with senior managers of companies seeking their support to sponsor their colleagues on development programmes or to publicly pledge their commitment to professional development by sponsoring staff (for example endowing a departmental chair) or facilities (such as funding a building). Another part of the week would be spent updating alumni on the work of the school and enlisting their support for new developments. Long-distance travel would probably be necessary. Time would also be set aside for interviews with journalists to encourage them to provide positive coverage to influence all constituents – current, past and potential students, clients and employers. In all of those activities the dean or director would be dependent upon the quality of support received from the officers who maintain networks, issue communications and create financial plans.

The above model is applicable for an autonomous or semi-autonomous school. Those more subject to the influence of state funding and to bargaining within the institution would require their dean to be somewhat less active externally, perhaps to a level of 40 per cent of available time. If such a proportion is regarded as excessive, bear in mind the importance of raising the unit's profile by joining and influencing national and international bodies and of the informal networking which goes on at such meetings. Even traditional activities such as external examining and speaking at conferences and seminars provide an opportunity to survey the field, which is becoming increasingly competitive, as the difficulties of recruiting top staff and raising performance in the RAE illustrate. This is background work which is distinct from the specific purposes of external relations work described above. What perhaps should guide the dean's, or others', efforts externally? Ensure that maximum benefit is derived from the time used. After all, there is a high opportunity cost in that time spent on external affairs is time lost in interacting with the staff of the unit and other colleagues in the institution. It also contains 'dead time' because of the travelling involved. Therefore, a high degree of preparation is essential: the unit should use its contacts to ensure that meetings and social events are planned by people who know the local situation. Well-briefed alumni or trusted counterparts at linked institutions are ideal. The purposes of visits and meetings are potentially varied, and might include the following activities on an overseas visit:

- negotiating with another provider to which the unit's programmes might be franchised, or with an agent who assists in student recruitment;
- recruiting students at undergraduate, taught Masters or postgraduate research levels;
- approaching companies which might sponsor their managers to take the unit's programmes;
- attending an educational exhibition to recruit students;
- interviewing applicants for places;

- encouraging the establishment or strengthening of a network of your unit's alumni;
- meeting prospective donors, whether alumni or others, to discuss mutual benefits;
- making or reinforcing contacts on behalf of colleagues in other faculties;
- attending carefully prepared meetings with influential parties, for instance foreign government departments, British Council offices, journalists, to raise the profile of your unit.

Visits within the UK also require careful planning which should enable maximum benefits to be derived from them. Debriefing after the event will also help the unit's staff and, where appropriate, central officers and colleagues in other faculties. A visit can produce a wealth of detailed impressions which will be of value to the institution in better understanding itself by better understanding its environment.

What approach should be used towards alumni? Are they not likely to be a variegated mass of people with whom it is expensive to communicate and who have no means of or interest in providing concrete support to their *alma mater*? This traditional UK attitude has been amended somewhat in recent years, but chiefly as a result of some HEIs' belief that there is money to be made from alumni relations. Sceptics assert that, other than at Oxford, Cambridge and some London colleges, the sums raised will scarcely cover the costs of the operation. Alumni activities tend to revolve around social events and reunions which are high on nostalgia and low on concrete significance.

At present there is much truth in these negative comments. However, as students begin to invest more of their own money in their higher education, they will become more discriminating and demanding and increasingly perceive a business relationship as well as an educational relationship with their HEI. The previous domination of the relationship by the state, which funded both the student and the institution in much larger measure than it will in future, made the notion of financial support seem alien. HEIs will use their small but precious funds from alumni to offer studentships on a variety of bases (academic merit, sporting or cultural excellence, means tested, ethnic origin, gender) in order to attract students who would otherwise go elsewhere. Such 'good causes' will be used to extend and enrich those scholarships and in time previous holders of them will feel honour bound, if they are encouraged to do so, to put back (pay back) some of what they received so that the virtuous circle may continue. Some HEIs still regard raising funds from alumni as a begging exercise, a somewhat shameful activity to be excused with cursed references to the government. They fear, even expect, abuse from outraged alumni who consider that they have no obligation to make contributions, particularly if they are taxpayers. This view may be superseded in the new more competitive climate of higher education. When the QAA has satisfied itself about minimum, threshold standards throughout the system, it will still be obvious – indeed, more obvious than ever – that some institutions' degrees are worth more than others'. Employers will become even more clear sighted about this phenomenon. A more business-like set of behaviours will become apparent:

- Undergraduate applicants will become more discriminating about their choice of course where they are academically strong enough to do so.
- Postgraduate numbers will rise as graduates aim to differentiate themselves from the mass of graduates, some of whom will have to take jobs for which a degree is not necessary.
- Postgraduate applicants will become even more selective about choice of course.
- Providers will compete through studentships (see above).
- Providers will also compete either on quality or on price.
- Providers will market their students and graduates more energetically and effectively to employers.
- Students and graduates will understand that they will gain added value from certain HEIs or courses, in terms of employment.
- Students and graduates will have a lifelong interest in the continued success of their department or HEI and will pay or donate to help enable it to maintain or improve its status.

Wise departments will invest time and effort now in their alumni. The effectiveness of their actions will be conditioned by the extent to which alumni loyalty is chiefly towards (a) the institution, (b) a college, or (c) the unit. Those in category (c) obviously constitute an attractive target for the units concerned. It is better to be active, even without the expectations of large gains in the short term. The first priority, apart from a reliable mailing list, is to keep the alumni well informed and feed them success stories. Most will be pleased to be contacted and we may not be far away from the time when they will be pleased to be asked for donations. They will soon criticize HEIs for lack of ambition in failing to generate fund-raising ideas and asking them for donations. Some business schools already experience criticism from students and alumni for failing to place display advertisements as frequently and prominently as they would wish – so much is their assessment of their future career bound up with the success of their institution. No wonder students are typically so loyal and positive about their educational experiences when meeting external assessors. Despite all these illustrations, leaders of some academic units show little interest in the world outside their campus. Even if income-generating opportunities are severely constrained by the nature of the market in their subject, much can be done. To take the example of the humanities department seeking to find £60,000–90,000 per annum in international tuition fees, its head should ask whether additional effort might enable it to double that recruitment and income without loss of quality. External effort could also be directed to the following activities:

- keeping abreast of quality assurance and thus enabling the department to lead, rather than to follow or be embarrassed by, developments;
- studying the employability of the department's graduates which entails contact with employers and alumni. Work in this area can enhance current students' prospects and be used later to reinforce student recruitment;
- surveying the field of staff in the subject, nationally and internationally, so that plans and approaches can be made as and when the department's age profile suggests the need for action;
- seeking publicity for newsworthy activities by students and staff. The department could be acting alone or in collaboration with other institutions (collaboration in itself is likely to be seen by the media as newsworthy).

By now an allowance of 40 per cent of time for external duties may not seem excessive!

The briefing of the dean is essential for all purposes. As the figurehead, the dean will be in constant demand to demonstrate the unit's official support for a range of relationships, initiatives and ceremonies. Some of these may be of minor importance to the unit and little more than irritations but at other times, the appearance and participation of the dean can make a real difference. For example, the head of the post-experience section has to negotiate contracts with board members of companies which will sponsor managers to undertake the unit's programmes. There are likely to be several decision points along the way at which the participation of a well-briefed dean, and perhaps his or her active participation in the presentation or in the subsequent delivery of the programme can have a major bearing on the outcome.

So various are the occasions on which the dean will be in demand that he or she must be given a proper briefing. Junior staff are apt to trust to the dean's superior wisdom and to assume that he or she will give the appropriate emphasis in the choice of what to say, and how and when to say it. This is not normally the case. In a large school, the dean can be expected to have an overview – but not more – of the significance of a particular activity. His or her colleagues must decide what outcomes they want and brief the dean, preferably in writing and well in advance, on background information and the purposes of the exercise. Failure to brief the dean which contributes to missed opportunities, offence being taken or confusion arising is not the fault of the dean who presides over the occasion, but of those colleagues who were responsible for the event. The dean generally fires the bullets which others have manufactured. A successful outcome is usually the result of good teamwork, not of inspired busking by the leader.

If the need to interact externally is predominant, is it advisable to appoint a dean or director from one of the professions concerned? A school which recruits a leader with a background in business has no difficulties in setting up an understanding with the person concerned: agree targets and perform to them. It is arguable that external constituents are more comfortable in dealing with someone who is more like them than with one of the faculty. It may be that people with a business background can grapple more readily with the changes in higher education which in fact parallel those in the business world:

- greater competition from academic and even from non-academic institutions, regionally, nationally and internationally;
- reduced resources from traditional sources, requiring increased effort to identify alternative sources of income;
- increased demand for customer service, placing pressure on the unit to deliver relevant provision with tangible benefits.

The associated skills, of strategic management, marketing research and development, financial management, and the management of professional support staff are most likely to be found in a business practitioner.

However, examples of successful transition from business to academia are relatively rare, particularly outside North America. There is only a small pool of successful business practitioners who have the background, temperament and desire to lead an academic institution. Deans and directors who emerge from the faculty not only have a head start in understanding and carrying the respect of academic colleagues as a result of their own efforts in teaching and research, but also are accustomed to the culture which responds to patience and incremental change rather than to top-down edicts. It is evident that success in fund-raising, for example, owes much to good research, patience and persistence rather than to extraordinary charisma. In that case, the academic is at least as likely as the business person to prove successful.

There are other risks in appointing a leader from 'the outside'. While it grabs the attention of the internal community, and proves the unit's serious intent, it also risks conveying a message that the needs of the unit are so special and different that they can effectively be disregarded at the institution's internal negotiating table. The unit may sign itself up for an externally determined destiny before it is ready to do so.

If the institution operates through many checks and balances, constraining the power of any leader to take actions rapidly – the 'unconscious conspiracy' described by Bennis (1989) – then the situation is likely to appear particularly frustrating to a senior manager from industry who is accustomed to determining his or her own destiny. There have been several examples of short-lived deanships which were terminated because 'they' constantly frustrated initiatives and set up obstacles to action.

Where a dean or director from a non-academic background is chosen, it is essential that he or she should take time to become fully appraised of the achievements, preferences and characteristics of the unit. The information will be needed anyway, for the purposes of promoting the unit but, more important, the leader must develop an instinctive understanding of which openings should be sought and which avoided. Nothing is more unwelcome to the faculty than having been committed by their leader to delivering a programme which they regard as beyond their scope or as unchallenging and unfulfilling. Not only must the dean bring in business, but also it must be the right kind of business.

Representing the unit internally

The skills required to represent the unit within the institution are substantially different from those needed externally. For this reason, the dean or director will have to be clear about how much time is available and what his or her priorities should be. For example, it would be perverse if a dean appointed for externally related skills were to set aside such work in favour of internal politics. The use of a deputy or associate deans or career administrative staff is the obvious way to solve the problem. Even a dean who commits to spending more than 50 per cent of time on the unit's external interests must devote considerable time to understanding and supporting colleagues and to chairing some key committees back at base. That still leaves a raft of other work, except in the case of wholly autonomous schools which have no parent body to be concerned about. Senior associates can handle issues of research policy, promotion and tenure, budget-setting and monitoring, representation on central committees and discussions with other faculties about collaboration. Some deans choose to involve themselves in some or all of these but they do so at the expense of the external roles which those who appointed them are likely to view as predominant.

The teamworking approach in the dean's office has many virtues, chiefly a division of labour which allows, for example, one senior professor to deal with the development and control of teaching programmes, another to lead research bids and encourage research output at an individual level and to deal with staffing issues, while a senior administrator implements a system of internal budgets and other resource-based issues such as IT provision and management of facilities.

It is easy to criticize such an arrangement. For example, is it not too resource intensive to involve four people, two of whom may be full-time, in the running of the unit? The actual and opportunity costs are excessive. However, these objections are appropriate only if the scale of operation is minor. If private income and discretionary expenditure form a tiny part of the whole, if staff and student numbers are low, if there is little complexity at the centre (for example because constituent cost centres manage almost everything through established appropriate systems), then a dean may be required only part-time and there may be no need to identify others to assist in the task.

It may also be objected that the use of multiple personnel will lead to confusion of objectives and tactics. It is undoubtedly the case that opponents take great delight in the appearance of disagreement between representatives of a unit, leading to their trying to adopt various divide-and-rule ploys. The unit's senior management team will naturally differ in some opinions but, having decided how to divide their responsibilities, they should allow the appropriate member of the group to lead the way, subject to the dean or director keeping an overall sense of direction. There is no necessary weakness in the team approach to internal issues, but there is a need for regular meetings or at least clear communications by other means to ensure that members of the unit know what each is trying to achieve. This activity is consistent with the briefing of the dean or director prior to public engagements. Too many academic units simply fail to take the trouble to hold briefings before important meetings – in some cases, they do not even know whether one of their representatives will be available to attend, let alone brief him or her so as to maximize the unit's prospects of achieving its objectives. Equally important, they fail to hold a debriefing at which the representative can report on the temperature of the political water. All too often, a second-hand oral report finds its way, distorted, to the dean's office or everyone has to await the appearance of the minutes of the meeting, which are likely to be useless several weeks after the event. Any unit which organizes itself in common-sense ways will greatly enhance its lobbying and bargaining power – if only because other units in higher education may be poorly set up to do likewise.

The senior management team, whether it is a self-contained group of three or four, or the centre of a more diffuse set of representatives, must trust and be trusted by the dean. Any incoming dean may 'inherit' some members of the group or otherwise have members imposed upon him or her, for example, by an electoral process. The dean should have the right of veto in cases where an election, say for associate dean, is likely to occur. It is in no one's interests for a dean and close associates to be unable to work together. If any member of the central team, including the dean, pursues a separate agenda, then trust is undermined. Meetings of the group are an opportunity to review progress, challenge assumptions and change tactics. Whatever the differences of opinion as to tactics, all members should be open about their intentions. Clearly the team requires a sufficiently broad base and enough independent thought to avoid the risk of 'group-think', but regular reinforcement of common objectives and mutual loyalty is desirable. The dean will wish to adjust the personnel in the group, not only to introduce those who are most attuned to his or her goals for the organization but also to strike a balance of personalities. An awareness of the principles of teamworking expounded by Belbin (1981, 1993) is particularly useful. Research in higher education in North America has suggested that successful leadership is likely to be associated with an effective team rather than with a single charismatic individual (Birnbaum 1988). The larger and more complex the enterprise, the more this is likely to be so.

In representing the unit internally, the dean – whether appointed from within or externally – is subject to contradictory pressures which are almost impossible to reconcile. In some institutions, the dean will be a member of a central management team with general responsibilities which extend beyond representation of a single academic area. The nightmare scenario in such a situation is that the dean may be forced to play a leading part in the downsizing of his or her own faculty. And yet it is at the time of worst cuts that strengths must be preserved for the future. If implemented by an uninformed person or group, cuts could fall in places which could permanently damage the prospects of revival. The dean will be uncomfortably aware of his or her remit to represent the whole of the unit (one might almost say 'right or wrong') and yet, confronted with factual evidence and the pressures affecting the whole institution, he or she may be virtually forced to choose between offering up sacrifices, or recommending 'equal misery for all' (a policy which might be acceptable at several levels) or resigning. Unless the dean is thick-skinned and unrelenting in supporting his or her unit, there will be times to accept defeats or to make uncomfortable compromises. Perhaps the only escape from that scenario is through the success of one or more units, and alternatively whole institutions, in generating income outside the state-funded arena which is subject to the relentless driving down of costs.

The normal mode for a faculty dean is to champion the cause of the unit, influencing those who decide agenda and set out models for the allocation of resources. Backroom influence is probably more effective than public table-thumping. Deans who indulge in the latter tactic quickly acquire a reputation for narrow-minded, short-sighted self-interest. The 'robber baron' approach to academic management may not be tolerated at all by senior management and, even if some early victories result, the dean may find that increasingly his or her views are discounted because they become predictably tedious to others. Militancy also makes it more difficult to create alliances, temporary and tactical or long term and fundamental, with other academic units. On some issues of principle, alliances can be effective. For example, an internal resource model may discriminate against departments which earn significant private income, in which case units such as the business school may make common cause with the engineering school to improve both units' chances of winning concessions.

In most academic institutions, there are a host of committees on which departmental representation is required. Deans are likely to find themselves in demand both as a representative and possibly also in a personal capacity, particularly for ad hoc bodies which are tasked with sorting out a complex problem. A dean who is unwilling to delegate or say no will tend to find that huge amounts of time are swallowed by good citizenship and 'service' which, to be blunt, must be a lower priority for a unit than both its external and its own internal activity. Frustration is magnified if the institution has been unable to create effective systems for its governance so that committees and working groups stumble across each other's paths and decisions are avoided or, worse, made but not implemented. Each unit owes it to itself to assess the choice of bodies on which it feels it should be represented, and then plan, probably through its senior management team, who should be identified for the roles concerned, making maximum use of each person's advantages in background knowledge and, if possible, interest in the subject. Again, procedures for the representative to be briefed and debriefed are an important means of judging the value of exercise. In these ways the unit may add value for the institution as a whole while protecting its own interests and without diverting significant amounts of time which should preferably be spent on research, teaching or other management duties.

The unit should assess and evaluate the total amount of resource being directed towards organizational matters. For example, it might be a mistake for the unit to nominate separate representatives for the institution's Finance and General Purposes Committee, dealing with 'macro' issues, and for its Budgeting and Monitoring Committee, dealing partly with 'micro' issues. Does it wish to retain eight separate departments when each head has to deal with all the business thrown at departments by central offices? Will it retain departments of only six to nine members when those are prone to severe problems arising from the taking of sabbatical leave, absences and succession to the headship? Larger departments enable the unit to reduce the duplication of administrative functions and to gain some modest economies of scale. The price to be paid may be the somewhat artificial yoking together of academic groups or individuals who may not be natural bed-fellows. This danger is often more apparent then real, since it can be small departments which suffer most from turf disputes between individual members. Every activity in a given school has a natural level of aggregation but sometimes political factors, history and the not-invented-here syndrome can prevent it from being found. Table 8.1 illustrates this for a fictional unit.

Whatever duties the dean is likely to encounter internally, financial responsibility is almost certain to be among them. In order to carry out those duties effectively, the dean must be confident in the commitment and ability of the budget-holders in the unit, in the accuracy of data supplied and in the support of central officers and bodies for actions the dean takes within the unit. The dean also needs to gain at least an overview of financial matters, from policy to detailed transactions. Actually getting hands-on or constantly intervening in detail is not appropriate because it is a misuse of expensive time and because it is possible to become blinded to the

Table 8.1 Natural level of aggregation

School	Department
Undergraduate admissions	Advanced undergraduate options
Undergraduate advice service	
Undergraduate work experience service	
	Postgraduate admissions
Marketing postgraduate programmes	Delivering postgraduate teaching
Timetabling postgraduate courses	Postgraduate work experience service
Doctoral programme, first year	Supervision of doctoral theses
	Scholarly research
Quality assurance procedures	Quality assurance monitoring
Purchasing	Estimating budgets
Negotiating budgets	Monitoring budgets

major issues by details. There are times when the ability rapidly to appraise a hastily tabled set of figures is an advantage. And yet deans rarely receive the induction and basic training they may need to carry out such a necessary task.

9

BENCHMARKING

Benchmarking and performance indicators

What are the meanings of 'benchmarking', an increasingly used term? It is being used within higher education in at least three contexts:

1 'Benchmarking is used to improve performance by understanding the methods and practices required to achieve *world-class* performance levels' (Camp 1995, added italics).
2 'The pursuit by organizations of enhanced performance by learning from the successful practices of others' (Holloway *et al*. 1998: 3).
3 In relation to quality assurance, the use of 'expert teams (to be known as subject benchmarking groups (SBGs)) ... to provide benchmark information by subject in the form of a statement of the standards of student attainment expected at the threshold level' (Quality Assurance Agency for Higher Education 1998: 10).

Hence, benchmarking is being used – confusingly – to refer to comparisons with levels of performance which are respectively world-class (1 above), successful (2 above), and at the threshold, that is the minimum acceptable (3 above).

Interest in benchmarking has always been present within higher education as a result of institutions' concerns about their teaching and its funding (for example numbers of funded students, percentage increase or decrease in level of annual funding) and about their own market position and share (numbers of applications per course, number of first-choice applications per course, A level entry scores, wastage and completion rates, percentage of students accommodated on campus, expenditure per student on computers and library, first-destination careers data, and so on). Most significantly, the peer review of performance of research and teaching (RAE and TQA) has taken on an overwhelming importance. Such data have come to be regarded as performance indicators which funding bodies, applicants, employers and other stakeholders could use to inform their choices of institution, course or employee. They have lent themselves to league tables which are published regularly and with at least the aura of official accuracy in respected media such as *The Times Higher*, *The Times* (*Good University Guide*) and the *Financial Times*. Other league tables, for aspects of performance in specific areas of provision such as the Master of Business Administration degree, appear in specialist journals or less predictably.

The unfair and misleading characteristics of most, if not all, such league tables have been professionally analysed by academics. Some blame the preoccupation with performance indicators upon the Thatcher government and its determination to reform higher education. And yet the exercises appeal to the competitive instincts which almost everyone shares. It is impressive to observe the child-like excitement of senior professors gathered together to receive a list of new RAE ratings!

Whatever one's opinion of the growing tendency to publicize measurements of performance, it must be acknowledged that accountability for the use of public funds is a legitimate interest. It is also helpful, and should arguably be mandatory, for each institution to study its own performance both against its own strategy and targets and against that of some of its peers/comparators/rivals. For understandable reasons, many people within academia are quite introspective, conscious of developments within their own institution but seldom aware of those developments' significance on a regional, national or international scale. For example, it might be important to know (not real cases):

- that yours is the only HEI in the region *not* offering a degree or diploma in Pest Control;
- that yours is the only HEI in the country offering a degree or diploma in the Physics of Manned Space Flight;
- that the 5 per cent increase to £1 million in funding from research contracts is only a modest cause for celebration: every other HEI exceeds your total;
- that the 5 per cent fall in your undergraduate applications compares with reductions of 12–25 per cent at all five of your closest comparator institutions.

Whether the news from benchmarking is good or bad, it can be vital to have it.

Benefits and pitfalls

How do you go about benchmarking? Referring back to the definitions above, (1) benchmarking your operations with those of the world leader is problematic. It may be impossible to determine who the world leader is, and perhaps there are marked differences according to sphere of activity, even within a single subject. More important, what will you learn? If yours is already an excellent department, then you may indeed gain much from the comparison, but otherwise you may be fruitlessly comparing unlike situations. If the world leader maintains its status through levels of funding which derive from its performance in assessments (for example from a 5* rating in research) or from its network of sponsors and alumni or from the presence of famous individual members of staff, you may glean little which is applicable to your own circumstances. A better benchmark may be the department which ranks above yours, having raised its profile in recent years despite having had to overcome some of the problems with which you are familiar. Despite the increased sense of competitiveness within the system, most academic staff are still willing to share information, receive visits and talk openly about their operations.

In definition (2), learning from success elsewhere is a reasonable expectation, particularly if – formally or informally – a benchmarking 'family' of like institutions can be formed. This is not always easy. For example, when a 1960s university identified a peer group of six similar-size, similar-age, similar-status institutions, it was discovered that one of its faculties had only two comparators in the peer institutions. It is most appropriate to benchmark within subjects. For example, compare your Chemistry Department with other Chemistry Departments, rather than your Chemistry Department with your History and Social Work Departments, because of the great differences in the environment facing each subject. It can be instructive to participate in a 'family' which contains at least one member to whose level of performance you might reasonably aspire (out of your grasp but not out of your sight) as well as some in similar circumstances to your own (preferably not your head-to-head competitors) and, to reciprocate your own aspiration, at least one member clearly performing at a level below your own.

What is the downside of undertaking this form of benchmarking? First, it requires time and effort, whether to collect and report facts and figures, or to take part in meetings to discuss them. Second, you are likely to disclose some confidential material which could become the subject of academic gossip. This danger is magnified if there is a risk of data being misunderstood and misrepresented; for example, you might franchise to another organization the teaching of some students who nevertheless count in your load model as if they were yours. This could lead to an official calculation that your student:staff ratio is much higher than it is in practice.

On the positive side, the benefits are likely to be considerable – and may make a new, direct and powerful contribution to your strategic planning and development and to making more persuasive the business plans which you place before institutional bodies and external bodies. At the operational level, you are likely to come across practices which you might adapt and adopt to improve the quality of services you provide and to become more effective or efficient.

In (3) above, the nature of the benchmarking is at the level of curriculum. It is a daunting experience to be presented with the wide diversity of purposes and practices in the UK's enlarged higher education sector. Nevertheless, in some subjects the institutions have recognized the importance of common cause and collaboration. For example, subject associations in history and English, to name just two, have proved robust and effective in response to the assessment of teaching quality, while the Association of Business Schools has promoted the collectivity of its member schools by lobbying activities armed with facts about the achievements of the sector, as set out in the booklet *Pillars of the Economy* (Association of Business Schools 1999).

What might a benchmarking exercise look like? Box 9.1 gives one illustration.

Box 9.1 Department or school benchmark

Staff profile

Number of academic staff
Percentage of classes taught by hourly paid staff
Number of staff with PhD, MPhil, MBA, MA/MSc, professional
    qualifications (such as chartered accounting bodies, Institute
    of Personnel and Development), BA/BSc
Research staff
Support staff: admin and technical

Student profile

Home and EU   Overseas   Total

Mode of study   %   Type of programme   %
Full-time (F/T)   Undergraduate
Sandwich (S/W)   Other advanced HND and professional
Part-time (P/T)   Postgraduate (taught)
Distance learning (D/L) Postgraduate (research)
Mature entrants (21+) as % of undergraduates

Taught programme profile   F/T   S/W   P/T

Main undergraduate programmes

Main postgraduate programmes

Main professional programmes

Resource base

Payroll and other direct expenditure

**Entrepreneurial activities   Gross revenue   % to school
                                to institution**

Revenue from in-company programmes
Income from research, development, consultancy

Research base

Rating in most recent RAE

No. and % of FTE staff entered

Staff currently research active and earmarked for entry into the
next RAE

Financial support reported to RAE per head from external
grants/contracts
1996   2001 (target)

PhD students graduating in the RAE period
1996   2001 (target)

Additional to the RA staff, another . . . are developing researchers

Distribution of RAE publications in various media:
1996   2001 (target)
Journals
Conference proceedings
Book chapters
Other

Organizational structure (attach a chart)

Other benchmarking exercises become possible when departments agree to share procedures as well as information. For example, if the whole 'family' agrees to adopt a common format and mode of administration for evaluation of teaching, it becomes possible to compare reliably the levels of student satisfaction on similar programmes at various institutions.

Some deans and their staff will be prepared to put effort into collecting and analysing data only if they lead to useful discussions with their counterparts. Even without the trappings of benchmarking, much informal contact already occurs. Indeed, since the enlargement of the sector it has become an expectation that like-minded groups, such as the Russell Group and the 94 Group, will share information in order to lobby the influential. There is even a danger that some, probably smaller, groups will act as cartels – perhaps to decide tuition fees in a way which will minimize any financial and political fall-out to themselves.

What can we learn from practice to date, both in industry and in the higher education sector? Benchmarking is becoming more widespread in both the public and private sectors, but its relative lack of a theoretical and conceptual base leads to a perception that it may prove to be a passing fad. Do the benefits outweigh the costs? If a benchmarking exercise is conducted as a snapshot for a specific purpose such as a departmental review, then probably not. It may be of interest to know that your department ranks fourth, fourteenth, tenth and eighth out of ninety in four measured areas of activity but such measures are unlikely to provide any signposts to further development. They may not even help you to understand why you are placed as you are. Effective benchmarking requires a commitment to processes of comparison and comparison of processes.

Research by the Open University Business School (Holloway *et al.* 1997, 1998) reports that benchmarking is most widespread in larger organizations and in the public sector – particularly in health, government and education – and in manufacturing and construction. Most concentrate on readily quantifiable activities measured against those in similar organizations (it is of course possible to benchmark with organizations in another industry). Benefits were seen to increase as organizations moved away from benchmarking for the purposes of measuring outputs towards benchmarking for understanding the processes which transform inputs to outputs.

An example of a benchmarking technique based upon a collection of objective data is given by Sarrico and Dyson (1998). The authors use data envelopment analysis (DEA) to evaluate performance in ten subjects on various dimensions. Performance in each subject is compared with that in peer institutions, supporting a 'portfolio'

approach to the management of HEIs which, like holding companies, consist of units in varying states of academic and financial health.

Ironically for a tool which is focused externally, benchmarking
provides data which are rich for the purposes of *introspection*. A vivid
picture emerges of how the organization applies its resources and
of how effective that application is in relation to its objectives.
Benchmarking lends itself naturally to internal studies of quality
summarized by the phrase 'continuous improvement' and to providing a catalyst for change. For example, it is more difficult to deny
that inefficiencies exist and to resist change if one is presented with
objective comparative information.

10

PREPARING TO LEAD, MANAGE – AND DEPART

Lack of training

There may be some well-managed institutions which engage in succession planning to identify in good time those who will take up leadership roles, or at least provide an induction programme to prepare them for the difficult tasks they will face. If so, the participants in such a process are suspiciously quiet. Most academic leaders report no experience of effective induction or training and, although some have attended courses on leadership, the content of those events is rarely sufficiently tailored to the requirements of working in higher education. 'Off the shelf' leadership courses tend to be extremely expensive, both directly and in time away, and often adapted to the needs of industry.

What are the effects of this absence of training? First, it inhibits the flow of volunteers for leadership positions. One has to be confident – or cavalier – to be undeterred by the absence of professional support in taking up a demanding role. Second, it makes more likely the appointment of insiders who know the system. Many deans quote their experience as associate deans or in other subordinate positions as most influential in guiding their own approach to leadership. Some draw on positive role models whereas others consider that a previous dean could show how one could go wrong! In summary, lack of training inhibits the field of candidates and promotes conservatism.

In their established positions, some deans take a grim satisfaction from the fact that their success, if such it be, has been achieved through their own observation, effort and skill. No one could recommend the absence of formal or informal development opportunities as a satisfactory situation when leadership is becoming more complex and demanding, particularly in higher education because it combines several characteristics which conspire to make the job more difficult. These include:

- professional autonomy, so you cannot order people around;
- resources reduced, so everyone has less time;
- resources reduced, so low morale is sometimes a problem;
- higher standards, or at least increased attention to standards, are demanded through research assessment and teaching quality assessment.

The issues surrounding development for leadership are well explored by Robin Middlehurst in her book *Leading Academics* (1993). She describes the barriers to effective development in terms of several 'cults in academic life' which suggest to those involved that training and development for leadership are unnecessary or an admission of inadequacy.

> The deficiences in competence, and the consequent lack of self-confidence by some senior staff and the lack of confident according of authority by their peers and subordinates can, I believe, be moderated by development programmes.
>
> Senior staff now have management responsibilities for the equivalent of large companies – hundreds of staff and millions of pounds and yet, despite the growth of management development for others, many resist the need to train for their new profession.
>
> Perhaps it is because few trained for their previous profession as teachers. Universities must overcome this amateurish anti-intellectualism. It is reminiscent of 19th century mill-owners.
>
> (Professor Ian McNay, formerly of
> Anglia Polytechnic University, letter to
> *The Times Higher*, 9 December 1994)

Leadership: what is required?

A report from the Committee of Vice-Chancellors and Principals: Universities and Colleges' Staff Development Agency (1994) identified five key areas of management which are required of leaders in academic institutions and in which they are capable of development:

- strategic
- operations
- resources/finance

- people
- information.

Management roles vary widely and can perhaps be categorized as follows:

- *Institutional managers'* roles are broad enough to encompass the whole institution, for example in finance, personnel, computing services and libraries. The holders of those roles are also unit managers (see next point).
- *Unit managers* implement a strategy for a defined area of activities and for the relationship of the unit to the rest of the institution. In some cases, holders of these roles also contribute to the evolution of policy. They are typically deans of schools or heads of administrative service functions.
- *Team managers* are to be found particularly in the functional areas (see above) of operations, resources/finance, people management and information management. Examples vary widely but include a professor heading a research group, a chief technician, a catering manager and an office manager.
- *Individuals as managers* include people who are managers without realizing it. They include lecturers who organize the delivery of taught courses and who select and present information to students, who set and mark examinations then analyse and present the results, who admit and advise students. Even the directly personal process of managing one's own time and priorities is an example of the management of resources.

In order to clarify thinking about development needs, the Green Paper presents the matrix shown in Box 10.1 for management/development training.

Box 10.1 Framework to describe development needs for managers at various levels

	Strategic	Operations	Resources/ finance	People	Information
Institutional managers					
Unit managers					
Team managers					
Individuals as managers					

The case of Virginia Tech

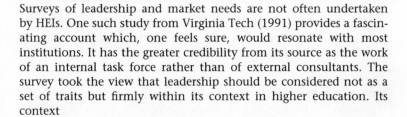

Surveys of leadership and market needs are not often undertaken by HEIs. One such study from Virginia Tech (1991) provides a fascinating account which, one feels sure, would resonate with most institutions. It has the greater credibility from its source as the work of an internal task force rather than of external consultants. The survey took the view that leadership should be considered not as a set of traits but firmly within its context in higher education. Its context

- is not hierarchical in that leadership is required at many levels from executive to supervisory. It is also devolved within academic units.
- combines leadership with management tasks: all leaders also have to be managers. The danger is that they may be faced with an excess of management tasks, thus blunting their effectiveness as leaders.
- requires leaders to provide a vision for the people in the organization.
- is culturally defined. Leaders affect shared values by nurturing, promoting or trying to change them.
- requires a role model. People expect their leaders to earn trust by showing integrity and competence.
- is classified by organizational analysts as, variously, a bureaucracy, a collegium, a political system and an organized anarchy.
- requires the ability to motivate, through nurturing or stimulating others, setting challenges, and using rewards – financial or other.
- requires leaders to represent the group to others.

In what ways has the culture developed and how does it impact on the roles of the leaders?

- There is normally conflict between academics and administrators.
- Institutional culture cannot be changed in the short term.
- Institutional cultures vary within the organization.
- HEIs have to be more responsive to external – political and financial – pressures.
- Decisions once made in a collegial context are now more often made in a bureaucratic context.
- Higher education depends upon the commitment of its employees.

When leaders were interviewed, it emerged that they

- are proud to be part of the institution;
- perceive little or no overall vision or shared values;
- feel loyal to a unit rather than to the institution as a whole;

- regard research as the most highly valued product/service (in another institution, this might be overshadowed by teaching while in others opinion might be evenly divided);
- doubt the ability of other units to achieve their goals;
- believe that rewards and accountability are inadequate in response to good and poor performances, respectively;
- believe that the system fails to reward teamwork;
- believe that central administration is not properly accountable for the services it provides;
- experience an excess of paperwork and bureaucracy, a lack of well-organized management information systems;
- regard feedback as negative rather than positive and that risk-taking is discouraged;
- notice a reluctance to take timely, difficult decisions;
- believe that departmental secretaries are the prime trainers of heads of department.

Does this sound familiar?

What qualities do members of the community (followers) seek in their leaders?

- vision: followers need to understand the organization's objectives in order to perceive purpose and impact in their own work;
- integrity;
- intervention only when required, not micro-management;
- active listening;
- assertiveness in dealing promptly with problems – and problem people;
- delegation, which is taken as a sign of trust;
- team-building to counterbalance institutional focus on individual effort and to promote collegiality;
- advocacy to represent the unit elsewhere;
- appraisal and feedback – justified praise and criticism are expected;
- personal communication to explain, to answer questions and to discuss changes;
- mediation to resolve disputes;
- political: followers wish leaders to be in touch with decision making and to be able to influence it.

What kind of development should be available to leaders? They regarded the following as most important:

- having access to a handbook containing advice and information for dealing with critical incidents;

- generating additional funding;
- managing stress;
- communicating effectively;
- creating a positive environment;
- rewarding good performance and dealing with unsatisfactory performance;
- developing appropriate attitudes to others;
- supporting innovative staff;
- initiating change rather than reacting to it;
- using time management;
- developing long-term goals for the unit;
- collaborating with other units;
- championing the unit;
- understanding the effect of words and actions on others;
- making and communicating timely decisions;
- building a culture of teamwork.

How can the prospects for a successful development programme be maximized? The leaders gave the following advice:

- Instructors with proven experience in working with managers should be used. Bring in external expertise.
- The programme should be voluntary and spread by its reputation.
- Training should start at the highest levels in the organization.
- Care should be taken to avoid raising false expectations.
- Academics and professional managers should be treated as distinct groups because of their differing career expectations.
- Instructors should act as facilitators and operate flexible, not highly structured, programmes.

Academic managers would prefer to learn on the job, perhaps with the support of a mentor. Learning from case studies and from others' experiences was preferred. They considered the most effective formats to be round-table discussion or fireside chats.

Academic leadership roles are doubly unattractive: in addition to the lack of preparation and development opportunities, there is normally an absence of support for re-entering mainstream academic life at the end of a period of headship. The least structured of such re-entry benefits would be a short period of sabbatical leave. It is difficult to see how HEIs can refuse such provision if they are serious about attracting able people to the varied leadership roles they require. Re-entry sabbaticals may be a 'sticking plaster' and the fundamental cure for the disease of inadequate leadership lies in a clearer

---

Box 10.2 A three-year leadership programme

Year 1
Induction (2 days):

- history, culture, procedures
- personal assessments, e.g. Myers-Briggs
  Type Inventory.

Module 1 on management skills (5 days):

- planning, setting priorities
- organizing, controlling, budgeting
- performance management
- decision making
- delegation
- communicating and explaining
- motivation
- time management
- active listening
- managing quality.

Year 2
Module 2 on organizational and networking skills (4 days):

- conflict resolution, mediating
- team-building
- building a sense of community
- representing the group
- working with various constituent groups.

Year 3
Module 3 on how organizations work (2 days):

- using skills from modules 1 and 2
- how to view problems in larger organizational context
- applying skills for managing change and problem solving.

---

enunciation of organizational goals. Organizational development specialists agree that optimum outputs are achieved when organizational and personal goals are congruent. In how many institutions are organizational and personal goals clear, even to senior officers? When they are not clear, leaders naturally tend to act in the interests of a faculty or a department, whose goals are somewhat more likely to be clear than those of the institution or, even more narrowly, in their personal interests. The imperative for the institution is surely to set up processes and make decisions which will provide incentives towards the behaviour it desires.

The survey concluded that the institution should begin a leadership development programme with a short residential event for no more than 30 of its most senior managers, with an in-built cascade in that afterwards each person would recommend a personal programme for him/herself and for one colleague. The deans should be brought together as a group in order to share ideas about good practice; an associated benefit might be a reduction in territorial behaviour. Generally, everyone gleaning information or ideas about management and leadership should be encouraged to give informal talks for colleagues with comparable responsibilities. Personalized leadership programmes should be created to identify a mentor for those new in post and to provide structured self-evaluation for leaders to monitor their performance. New heads of academic and administrative units require a thorough three-year programme which would take them from an induction into the history, culture and procedures of the institution through modules on management skills and organizational and networking skills to a module on how organizations work (see Box 10.2).

At a lower level in the organization, first-line supervisors should experience a planned development programme. They directly affect the performance and morale of large numbers of employees and should be supported in their roles of communicating standards and building team performance in a wide range of service functions.

Challenges remain

Pressure of time – which may be translated in terms of other things being more important or more urgent – is the chief enemy of development activities. The ultimate challenge for staff developers, working alongside the most senior managers, is to create and sustain a programme of development appropriate to the needs of each institution and the people who work at different levels within it, such that most will no longer say that they cannot afford the time to attend.

Has the situation improved in response to the pressures to manage HEIs more effectively since the above major surveys were carried out? Evidently not, according to Bone and Bourner (1998). Their survey of a sample of UK universities found that only half are running management development programmes for heads of department and those in more senior roles. The evidence is that HEIs are undertaking less development provision for their managers than is the case in companies. This is ironic in view of educational mission and institutions' exhortations to companies to use academic expertise to upgrade the development of their managers.

Provision tends to founder on senior managers' reluctance to take part in formal management development and, in some institutions, on lack of support from the top.

> Managers themselves, particularly those at head of department level, were ambivalent about the issue of management development. Some saw themselves mainly as academic leaders, with a clear mission to promote their subject area by participating in, and encouraging, others to research. They did not want to be managers in the usual sense of that term. Others (a minority) saw that the nature of higher education had changed and that some management skills such as financial planning and effective recruitment were of increasing importance and needed to be developed.
>
> (Bone and Bourner 1998: 294)

Most programmes in HEIs tend to deal with knowledge and skills for purposes such as financial management, appraisal, leadership, recruitment and managing change. Development programmes on understanding systems, on creativity and on working across organizational boundaries are much less common. Bone and Bourner (1998) suggest that a greater use could be made of mentoring and of action learning sets in order to achieve more ambitious outcomes. Such provision could be led by internal staff, such as staff development officers, and would be relatively inexpensive. This recommendation differs from the preference expressed at Virginia Tech (1991) for external expertise to launch the process.

Bone and Bourner (1998) found that one-third of their respondents had achieved, or were working towards, Investors in People status. However, it appeared that there is a weak relationship between the espoused position on staff development, as expressed in a mission statement, and actuality. That is not to say that actuality always lags behind declared policy – it can be the reverse – but Investors in People does require a match between organizational objectives and the staff development work which is designed to achieve them.

One is left with an overwhelming feeling that something better and larger can, and should, be done. Improved provision could be the engine to drive forward better management within faculties, better relationships between faculties and better management of whole institutions.

Knowing when to quit and life after deaning ▮

> What comes after being a dean? – I sometimes worry about this
> (David Asch, former Dean of the Open University
> Business School quoted in European Foundation
> for Management Development 1998: 33)

Returning to the faculty, retiring, moving into consultancy or into another avenue of academic management are not the only options. However, none has made a greater splash than Robert James Waller, former Dean of Business at the University of Northern Iowa, who went on to write the best-selling novel *The Bridges of Madison County*.

One experienced dean whom I interviewed in 1994 took the view that after seven or eight years, one's 'political capital' is used up and the rhetoric that may have once inspired colleagues sounds stale. He was as good as his word. Three years later, and on his own cue, he moved outwards and upwards in the management of higher education.

> As far as I'm concerned, the rule of thumb is to serve no more than two terms (ten years) as dean, or you'll experience diminishing returns for your efforts . . . The dean has to be able to articulate a vision, and if your constituencies can't see the star you're shooting for, it's time for you to go.
> (Robert Sullivan, former Dean of the
> Graduate School of Industrial Administration
> at Carnegie Mellon University)

> The days of serving as dean for 15 to 20 years are gone. The pressure is too much. I'd say ten years is the maximum amount of time for a dean today . . . It's important to step down while people still think you're doing a good job – retire two years earlier than you originally projected.
> (Tom Bausch, former Dean of Business
> at Marquette University)

Colin Blaydon, former Dean at the Amos Tuck School of Business Administration, Dartmouth College, says there is a natural law of longevity for business school deans, and that law says seven years is long enough. Re-entering the faculty can prove difficult: 'You must stand back and force yourself to stay out of the new dean's way' (Tom Bausch).

The pace of life is so different. And if you weren't perceived as being very successful as a dean, it's almost an embarrassment to return to the faculty. But, faculty tend to revere successful deans who choose to return to the faculty. These deans have a special role to play in the life of the school.

(Robert Sullivan)

The process of teaching is like riding a bike, but your field changes. Finance is a high-octane field and it would take a while for me to get back up to speed. I don't want to break all the rules (regarding faculty standards) I'd put into place when I was dean. It was better for me to make a clean break.

(Dick West, former Dean of the Stern School
of Business at New York University)

I'd urge an ex-dean to carry a fair share of the workload as far as teaching and student advising are concerned.

(Tom Bausch)

As I've observed it, the difficult part for academics returning to the faculty is getting back into the swing of research.

(John McKinnon, former Dean of the
Babcock School of Business at
Wake Forest University)

Returning or moving into business careers is challenging but opinions vary as to whether the roles are tougher, or less tough, than being dean.

In business, people don't have time for discussing ideas just for the sake of intellectual stimulation. They always want to know if an idea can make money for the company. In business, implementing ideas is the important issue . . . As dean, you don't have a lot of leverage over the faculty. And in industry, you have far more leverage (over those who support you) but more is expected of you . . . In industry you see financial rewards; in academia the rewards are intellectual.

(Nancy Jacobs, former Dean of Business
at the University of Washington)

A move into the management of other areas of higher education is perhaps the most straightforward. Subject background can play an important part. Whilst business school deans should understand the complexities of the corporate management of an academic enterprise and should have built up working relationships with external constituencies such as companies, it may be scientists who have the inside track with research councils and high-technology companies, and possibly social scientists or humanities people who have the best governmental and political networks.

(AACSB – The International Association for
Management Education 1995: 3–10)

BIBLIOGRAPHY

AACSB – The International Association for Management Education (1995) *Newsline*, summer: 3–10.

Association of Business Schools (1999) *Pillars of the Economy: Developing World Class Management Performance – The Contribution of UK Business Schools to the Economy 1999*. London: Association of Business Schools.

Belbin, R. M. (1981) *Management Teams: Why They Succeed or Fail*. London: Heinemann.

Belbin, R. M. (1993) *Team Roles at Work*. Oxford: Butterworth Heinemann.

Bennis, W. (1989) *Why Leaders Can't Lead: The Unconscious Conspiracy Continues*. San Francisco, CA: Jossey-Bass.

Bensimon, E. M. (1989) The meaning of 'good presidential leadership': a frame analysis, *Review of Higher Education*, 12(2): 107–23.

Bensimon, E. M. (1991) The social processes through which faculty shape the image of a new president, *Journal of Higher Education*, 62(6): 637–60.

Bensimon, E. M. (1993) New presidents' initial actions: transactional and transformational leadership, *Journal for Higher Education Management*, 8(2): 5–17.

Birnbaum, R. (1986) Leadership and learning: the college president as intuitive scientist, *Review of Higher Education*, 9(4): 381–95.

Birnbaum, R. (1988) *How Colleges Work: The Cybernetics of Academic Organization and Leadership*. San Francisco, CA: Jossey-Bass.

Birnbaum, R. (1992) Will you love me in December as you do in May? Why experienced college presidents lose faculty support, *Journal of Higher Education*, 63(1): 1–25.

Bolton, A. R. (1995) A rose by any other name: TQM in higher education, *Quality Assurance in Education*, 3(2): 12–18.

Bolton, A. R. (1996) The leadership challenge in universities: the case of business schools, *Higher Education*, 31: 491–506.

Bolton, A. R. (1997) How to succeed in business school leadership by really trying, *Perspectives*, 1(2): 62–5.

Bone, A. and Bourner, T. (1998) Developing university managers, *Higher Education Quarterly*, 52(3): 283–99.

Camp, R. C. (1995) *Business Process Benchmarking: Finding and Supplementing Best Practices*. Milwaukee, WI: ASQC Quality Press.

Carnall, C. A. (1990) *Managing Change in Organizations*. London: Prentice Hall.

Cave, M., Hamney, S., Henkel, M. and Kogan, M. (1997) *The Use of Performance Indicators in Higher Education: The Challenge of the Quality Movement*. London: Jessica Kingsley.

Clark, B. R. (1998) *Creating Entrepreneurial Universities: Organisational Pathways of Transformation*. Paris: International Association of Universities Press and Elsevier Science.

Cohen, M. D. and March, J. G. (1974) *Leadership and Ambiguity: The American College President*. New York: McGraw-Hill.

Committee of Vice-Chancellors and Principals: Universities and Colleges' Staff Development Agency (1994) *Higher Education Management and Leadership: Towards a National Framework for Preparation and Development*, Green Paper no. 9. London: UCo SDA.

Cowen, R. (1991) The management and evaluation of the entrepreneurial university: the case of England, *Higher Education Policy*, 4(3): 9–13.

Doz, Y. L. and Hamel, G. (1998) *Alliance Advantage: The Art of Creating Value through Partnering*. Boston, MA: Harvard Business School Press.

Eriksson, C. B. (1998) *What Does it Take to Lead a Department?* Reports in English from the Quality Group 5, May, Uppsala University.

European Foundation for Management Development Forum (1998) Educating management for the new competitive age, *European Foundation for Management Development Forum*, 98(1): 30–49.

Fielden, J. and Lockwood, G. (1973) *Planning and Management in Universities*. London: Chatto and Windus.

Finlay, P. N. and Gregory, G. (1994) A management support system for directing and monitoring the activities of university academic staff, *Journal of the Operational Research Society*, 45: 641–50.

Fortune (1994) What is killing the business school deans of America? *Fortune*, 130(3): 8 August.

Graduate Management Admissions Council (1997) An interview with Robert H. Atwell, *Selections*, spring/summer: 29–35.

Graduate Management Admissions Council (1998) An interview with Dean Joseph B. White, *Selections Magazine*, winter: 22–7.

Gray, H. L. (1989) Resisting change: some organisational considerations about university departments, *Educational Management and Administration*, 17: 123–32.

Higson, H., Filby, J. and Golder, V. (1998) A critique of a model for an academic staff activity database developed to aid a department in strategic and operational decision-making, *Perspectives*, 2(1): 28–32.

Holloway, J., Hinton, M., Mayle, D. and Francis, G. (1997) *Why Benchmark? Understanding the Processes of Best Practice Benchmarking*, working paper 97/8. Milton Keynes: Open University Business School.

Holloway, J., Francis, G., Hinton, M. and Mayle, D. (1998) *Making the Case for Benchmarking*, working paper 98/5. Milton Keynes: Open University Business School.

Jarratt Report (1985) *Report of the Steering Committee for Efficiency Studies in Universities*. London: Committee of Vice-Chancellors and Principals of the UK Universities (CVCP).

Johnes, J. and Taylor, J. (1990) *Performance Indicators in Higher Education*. Buckingham: Society for Research into Higher Education and Open University Press.

King, M. and Pile, B. (1997) *Administering a Model of the Activities of University Academic Staff*, working paper. Loughborough: Loughborough University.

Lefell, L. G., Robinson, J. F., Harshberger, R. F., Krallman, J. D. and Frary, R. B. (1991) Assessing the leadership culture at Virginia Tech, in L. A. Sherr and D. J. Teeter (eds) *Total Quality Management in Higher Education, New Directions for Institutional Research 71*. San Francisco, CA: Jossey-Bass.

Lorange, P. (1988) Stimulating strategic direction setting in professional groups: the case of an academic department, *Advances in Strategic Management*, 5: 299–320.

Macdonald, R. (1997) How to survive as Head of Department, in J. Richards (ed.) *Uneasy Chairs: Life as a Professor*. Lancaster: Unit for Innovation in Higher Education, Lancaster University.

Middlehurst, R. (1989) Leadership and higher education, *Higher Education*, 19: 353–60.

Middlehurst, R. (1993) *Leading Academics*. Buckingham: Society for Research into Higher Education and Open University Press.

Miller, H. D. R. (1995) *The Management of Change in Universities: Universities, State and Economy in Australia, Canada and the United Kingdom*. Buckingham: Society for Research into Higher Education and Open University Press.

Mintzberg, H. (1973) *The Nature of Managerial Work*. New York: Harper and Row.

Mintzberg, H. (1994) *The Rise and Fall of Strategic Planning*. Englewood Cliffs, NJ: Prentice Hall.

Myers, I. B. and McCaulley, M. H. (1985) Manual: *A Guide to the Development and Use of the Myers-Briggs Type Indicator*. Palo-Alto, CA: Consulting Psychologists Press.

Neumann, A. (1989) Strategic leadership: the changing orientations of college presidents, *Review of Higher Education*, 12(2): 137–51.

Neumann, A. (1990) Making mistakes: error and learning in the college presidency, *Journal of Higher Education*, 611: 386–407.

Neumann, A. and Bensimon, E. M. (1990) Constructing the presidency: college presidents' image of their leadership roles: a comparative study, *Journal of Higher Education*, 61(6): 678–701.

Newby, M. (1997) Being a dean, in J. Richards (ed.) *Uneasy Chairs: Life as a Professor*. Lancaster: Unit for Innovation in Higher Education, Lancaster University.

Quality Assurance Agency for Higher Education (1998) *Higher Quality*, 1(3): 10–12.

Sarrico, C. S. and Dyson, R. G. (1998) *Performance Measurement in UK Univer-*

sities: The Institutional Perspective, research papers no. 286. Warwick: Warwick Business School.

Sherr, L. A. and Teeter, D. J. (eds) (1991) *Total Quality Management in Higher Education, New Directions for Institutional Research 71*. San Francisco, CA: Jossey-Bass.

Smith, K. R. (1996) Faculty leadership and change in higher education, *Selections*, winter: 19–27.

Temple, P. and Whitchurch, C. (1989) *Strategic Choice: Corporate Strategies for Change in Higher Education*. Manchester: Conference of University Administrators/Touche Ross.

Thomas, H. G. (1997) The unexpected consequences of financial devolution, *Higher Education Review*, 29(3): 7–21.

Virginia Tech (1991) *Report of the University Task Force on Leadership Development*, document no. PDS 81.

Warner, D. and Palfreyman, D. (eds) (1996) *Higher Education Management: The Key Elements*. Buckingham: Society for Research into Higher Education and Open University Press.

Wholihan, J. T. (1990) Business dean turnover: causes and consequences, *Selections*, autumn.

Williams, G. (1992) *Changing Patterns of Finance in Higher Education*. Buckingham: Society for Research into Higher Education and Open University Press.

INDEX

CHANGING ACADEMIC WORK
DEVELOPING THE LEARNING UNIVERSITY

Elaine Martin

Higher education has changed enormously in recent years. For instance, it now serves a more diverse range of students and is under closer government scrutiny and control. There is consequently a significant number of academics who are uneasy with current values and practices and who work with them reluctantly. Universities may speak publicly of efficiency and effectiveness but they cannot function successfully if their academic staff are disillusioned.

Changing Academic Work explores the competing tensions in contemporary work: the need to balance individualism with collaboration; accountability with reward; a valuing of the past with preparation for the future. The aim is to help staff build a contemporary university which is as much a learning organization as an organization about learning. Elaine Martin develops a set of simple but sound principles to guide academic work and, through case study material, she provides engaging and convincing illustrations of these principles in action. She offers insight and guidance for academic staff at all levels who wish to make their working environment more satisfying and productive.

Contents
Preface – Changes in academic work – Experiences of change in academic work – Learning and teaching in higher education – Organizational change and learning organizations – Finding a way forward – Visions and missions and reality – Collaboration and independence – Accountability and reward – Encouraging change: valuing the past, preparing for the future – A final word: a better working life – Bibliography – Index.

192pp   0 335 19883 X (Paperback)   0 335 19884 8 (Hardback)

THE INCOME GENERATION HANDBOOK
A PRACTICAL GUIDE FOR EDUCATIONAL INSTITUTIONS

David Warner and Charles Leonard

'Income generation' has become part of a new language in education circles, alongside such terms as 'marketing', 'customer-led', and 'enterprise'. This book sets out the policy context and theoretical framework for income generation, and provides practical guidance on how to succeed in this innovative and complex area. It covers the whole field including internal and external marketing opportunities, running short courses, student recruitment, delivery models, sponsorship and other sources of funds, financial and quality control. The core chapter describes over a hundred tried and tested income generation projects.

It is written by two active practitioners in the field of income generation, and will be a constant reference and stimulus for all educational managers.

Contents
What is income generation? – Home student recruitment – The anatomy of a short course – Financial arrangements – Delivery models – Opportunities for income generation – Obtaining sponsorship – Sources of funds – Research – Operating an internal business – The art of successful delivery – Bibliography – Index.

160pp   0 335 15718 1 (Paperback)   0 335 15719 X (Hardback)

Faculty